ARIZONA, THE GRAND CANYON & EVERYTHING IN BETWEEN

(This guide also features Phoenix, Tucson, Sedona, Flagstaff, and their surroundings.)

A Travel Guide to the Heart of the Southwest

Harrison Walshaw

Disclaimer:

This Arizona Travel Guide contains general information only. While efforts are made to provide accurate and up-to-date information, there are no express or implied representations or warranties regarding the completeness, accuracy, reliability, suitability, or availability of the guide or the information, products, services, or related graphics it contains. Any reliance you place on such information is therefore strictly at your own risk. In no event will the publisher be liable for any loss or damage, including without limitation, indirect or consequential loss or damage, or any loss or damage whatsoever arising from loss of data or profits arising out of, or in connection with, the use of this guide. Please be aware that the information provided in this guide is subject to change, and it is advisable to confirm with official sources and local authorities before making travel plans or decisions.

We hope this travel guide enriches your exploration of Arizona and its myriad wonders, from the majestic Grand Canyon to the vibrant cities and hidden desert gems. May your journey through the heart of the Southwest be filled with adventure and discovery.

Cover Image Credit ©

Sean Pavone via Canva, https://www.canva.com/photos/MADesH948Y4/

Contents

ARIZONA

THE GRAND CANYON STATE
WELCOMES YOU

Welcome to Arizona, a land of diverse landscapes and rich cultural heritage. This guide will take you on a journey through the Grand Canyon State, a place where the majestic beauty of nature meets a vibrant cultural scene. From the awe-inspiring depths of the Grand Canyon to the serene red rocks of Sedona, and the bustling urban centers of Phoenix and Tucson, Arizona offers a variety of experiences for every traveler.

As you explore this guide, you'll find yourself immersed in a state that is not only home to one of the world's natural wonders but also boasts a wealth of other natural and cultural attractions. You'll learn about the best spots to experience the grandeur of the Grand Canyon, the artistic and spiritual havens of Sedona, and the historical richness of Tucson.

Arizona's landscape is an exciting playground for outdoor enthusiasts, offering everything from hiking and rafting to more leisurely pursuits like golf and wine tasting. The state's unique blend of Native American, Mexican, and Western influences is evident in its cuisine, offering flavors that are as varied as its geography.

In this guide, you'll find useful tips for places to visit, outdoor activities to enjoy, and insights into Arizona's unique cultural heritage. Whether you're watching a sunset over the Grand Canyon, exploring ancient ruins, or enjoying the local cuisine, your journey through Arizona is sure to be filled with memorable experiences.

Prepare for an adventure in a state where every corner offers something new to discover. Welcome to Arizona – a place where adventure and discovery await at every turn.

Geography and Climate

Arizona, a state characterized by its extraordinary geographical diversity, stretches across the southwestern United States. The state's topography is a remarkable blend of deserts, plateaus, and mountain ranges, creating a landscapes that are as varied as they are stunning.

In the southern region of Arizona lies the expansive Sonoran Desert. This desert is not only a vast expanse of sand and heat but is also teeming with life. It's home to the iconic Saguaro cactus, a symbol of the American Southwest. The Sonoran Desert's terrain is punctuated by low-lying valleys and sprinkled with small mountain ranges, offering a stark yet captivating beauty. The climate here is typified by extremely hot summers, where temperatures can soar well above 100°F (38°C), and mild winters that attract visitors from colder regions.

Moving northwards, the geography undergoes a dramatic transformation. The Colorado Plateau, a massive highland region, dominates the northern part of the state. This plateau is a marvel of geology, characterized by its layered bands of colorful rock formations, deep canyons, and stark mesas. The Grand Canyon, one of the world's most awe-inspiring natural wonders, is carved into the heart of this plateau by the Colorado River. The climate here contrasts sharply with the south, as the higher elevation results in cooler temperatures. Winters bring considerable snowfall, particularly in the higher altitudes, turning the plateau and mountain regions into winter wonderlands.

The San Francisco Peaks, a volcanic mountain range near Flagstaff, are among the most prominent features of the northern Arizona landscape. These peaks, including the state's highest point, Humphreys Peak, are remnants of an eroded stratovolcano and are sacred to several Native American tribes. The area around these peaks experiences a mountain climate, with cool summers and snowy winters, offering opportunities for skiing and snowboarding.

Across these diverse regions, Arizona's climate plays a significant role in shaping the state's natural environment. The arid desert conditions in the south have given rise to unique adaptations in flora and fauna, while the cooler, more temperate climate in the north supports a completely different set of ecosystems. This contrast not only makes Arizona a fascinating study in geography and climatology but also a playground for a wide range of outdoor activities and ecological exploration.

Brief History and Culture

Arizona's history is a vivid mosaic of various cultures and epochs, each leaving a distinct imprint on the state's identity. Its story begins long before European exploration, deeply anchored in the rich traditions and histories of Native American tribes.

The earliest inhabitants of what is now Arizona were Native Americans, with evidence of their presence dating back thousands of years. Prominent tribes such as the Navajo, Hopi, and Apache, among others, have shaped much of the state's early history. These tribes developed complex societies, known for their intricate art, sophisticated agricultural practices, and deeply spiritual belief systems. Their legacy is evident in the numerous archaeological sites found throughout the state, including the well-preserved cliff dwellings at Canyon de Chelly and the ancient pueblo ruins at Wupatki National Monument.

The arrival of Europeans marked a turning point in Arizona's history. Spanish explorers and missionaries first ventured into the region in the 16th century, seeking to spread Christianity and claim new territories for the Spanish Empire. Spanish colonialism left a lasting impact, particularly in the introduction of Catholicism, which is still evident in the state's historic missions like the Mission San Xavier del Bac near Tucson.

In the 19th century, Arizona became a part of Mexico following Mexico's independence from Spain in 1821. However, this era was short-lived. The Mexican-American War in the 1840s resulted in Mexico ceding much of what is now the American Southwest, including Arizona, to the United States in 1848 under the Treaty of Guadalupe Hidalgo. Arizona's admission as a U.S. territory and later a state (in 1912) ushered in the era of the American West, characterized by mining booms, cattle ranching, and the expansion of the railroad.

Throughout the 20th century, Arizona experienced significant growth and change. The state's economy diversified, moving beyond mining and agriculture to include manufacturing, tourism, and technology. This period also saw an increase in population and cultural diversity, with people from all over the United States and beyond making Arizona their home.

Today, Arizona's cultural landscape is as diverse as its history. The influence of Native American tribes is still strongly felt in the state's art, music, and festivals. These cultures are celebrated in events like the annual Pow Wow at the Heard Museum in Phoenix, which showcases traditional dances, music, and art. The Spanish and Mexican legacies are also prominent, especially in Arizona's southwestern architecture, cuisine, and cultural celebrations like Cinco de Mayo.

Overview of Major Cities

Arizona's major cities boast diversity and dynamism mirroring the state's varied landscapes, each offering unique experiences, cultural richness, and an overabundance of attractions.

Based on Arizona's Demographics by Cubit (https://www.arizona-demographics.com), the top 10 cities by population are as follows:

1. Phoenix - 1,609,456	2. Tucson - 541,033	3. Mesa - 503,390
4. Chandler - 275,618	5. Gilbert - 267,267	6. Glendale - 248,083
7. Scottsdale - 240,537	8. Peoria - 191,292	9. Tempe - 181,005
10. Surprise - 145,591		

Additionally, notable destinations such as Grand Canyon Village, Flagstaff, and Sedona contribute to the state's allure:

- Grand Canyon Village: 1,914
- Flagstaff: 76,177
- Sedona: 9,739

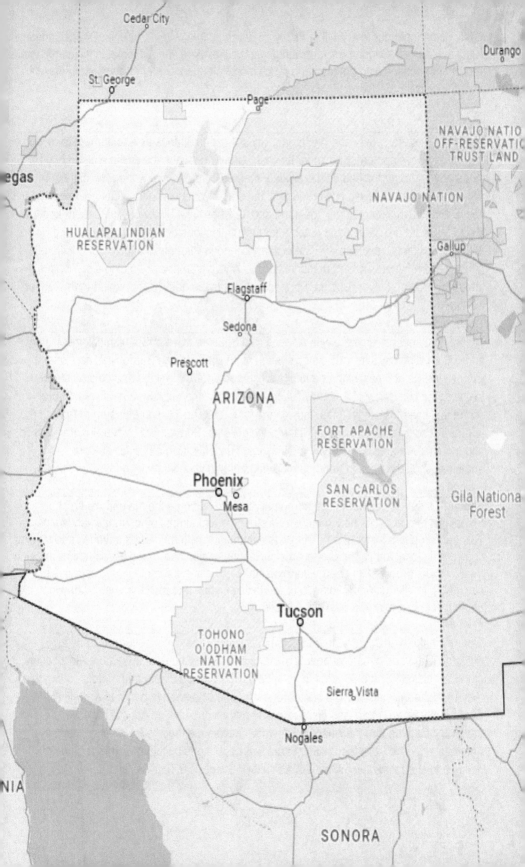

In this guidebook, our focus will primarily be on attractions within Phoenix, Grand Canyon, Tucson, Flagstaff, Sedona and surroundings. We'll explore various aspects including hotel accommodations, dining options, and much more to enhance your experience in these vibrant locales.

Phoenix

Phoenix, the state capital and the largest city in Arizona, stands as a testament to modern growth and development. Known for its vast, sprawling layout, the city is a blend of urban modernity and natural beauty. The skyline, marked by modern skyscrapers, hints at the city's role as the economic powerhouse of the state. Phoenix is also a cultural hotspot, boasting an array of museums, theaters, and galleries. The Phoenix Art Museum and the Heard Museum are particularly notable for their collections of contemporary art and Native American artifacts, respectively. The culinary scene in Phoenix is a fusion of traditional Southwestern flavors and international cuisine, offering an array of dining experiences. As the transportation hub of Arizona, Phoenix serves as the gateway to exploring the rest of the state.

Tucson

Tucson, the second-largest city in Arizona, is a treasure trove of Spanish colonial history and culture. The city's historic districts, such as El Presidio and Barrio Histórico, offer a glimpse into its rich past with beautifully preserved adobe buildings and colorful streets. Home to the University of Arizona, Tucson is vibrant and youthful, with a lively cultural scene that includes art galleries, music, and festivals. The Tucson Museum of Art and the annual Tucson Gem and Mineral Show are highlights. Surrounded by the Sonoran Desert and mountain ranges like the Santa Catalinas, Tucson is also a hub for outdoor enthusiasts, offering hiking, mountain biking, and bird watching.

Sedona

Sedona's fame comes from its extraordinary natural setting – the majestic red rock formations that encircle the town create a stunning and almost otherworldly landscape. This backdrop has fostered a thriving arts community, with numerous galleries and studios showcasing local and international artists. Sedona is also known for its spiritual allure, with many visitors drawn to its energy vortexes and wellness retreats. Outdoor activities are plentiful, with hiking trails leading to breathtaking vistas, and the Oak Creek Canyon offering scenic drives and picnicking spots.

Flagstaff

Situated in the high country near the San Francisco Peaks and the Grand Canyon, Flagstaff is a blend of natural beauty, historic charm, and outdoor adventure. Its location along the historic Route 66 adds to its appeal, with vintage diners and motels dotting this famous highway. Flagstaff is a center for astronomical research, home to Lowell Observatory where Pluto was discovered. The city's proximity to natural attractions like the Grand Canyon and the Arizona Snowbowl makes it a favorite for hikers, skiers, and nature lovers. The vibrant downtown area, with its historic buildings, offers a range of dining and shopping options, as well as cultural events and festivals.

Best Times to Visit

Deciding the best time to visit Arizona hinges on the specific regions you wish to explore and the activities you have in mind. The state's diverse geography means weather conditions can vary greatly from one area to another.

Spring (March to May)

- Spring is an exceptional time to visit most of Arizona. The weather is generally mild and pleasant, with daytime temperatures comfortable for outdoor activities.
- In the southern desert regions, including Phoenix and Tucson, the landscape comes alive with a spectacular display of wildflowers.
- The northern regions, including the Grand Canyon and Flagstaff, offer cooler but enjoyable weather, perfect for hiking and exploring.

Summer (June to August)

- Summer in Arizona, particularly in the desert areas, is known for its extreme heat, with temperatures often soaring above 100°F (38°C).
- This is a great time to visit the higher elevations in the north, such as the San Francisco Peaks and the White Mountains, where the climate is significantly cooler and conducive to outdoor activities like hiking, mountain biking, and fishing.
- Evening events, such as outdoor concerts or night markets, are popular in the cities during summer.

Fall (September to November)

- Fall brings cooler temperatures and a change of scenery, especially in the northern parts of Arizona. The foliage in areas like Oak Creek Canyon near Sedona transforms into vibrant hues of orange, red, and yellow.
- This season is ideal for outdoor activities across the state, from hiking in the deserts to exploring the high country.
- Fall festivals and events, celebrating everything from art to local cuisine, are abundant during this time.

Winter (December to February)

- Southern Arizona enjoys mild and pleasant winters, making it a perfect time for golfing, hiking, and exploring the desert landscapes.
- Northern Arizona transforms into a winter wonderland, attracting visitors for skiing, snowboarding, and other winter sports at resorts like Arizona Snowbowl near Flagstaff.
- The cooler weather also makes visiting cultural attractions in the cities more comfortable.

Travel Essentials

When packing for Arizona, it's important to consider the varied climate and diverse activities the state offers. Here are some essentials that should be on every traveler's checklist:

Clothing

Summer: Opt for lightweight, breathable fabrics to stay comfortable in the heat. Think cotton or moisture-wicking materials. Include shorts, t-shirts, and long-sleeved shirts for sun protection.

Winter: Bring layers that can be easily added or removed as temperatures fluctuate. This includes a mix of light sweaters, jackets, and possibly a warm coat if visiting northern regions.

Year-Round: Regardless of the season, it's wise to pack a few layers, such as a light jacket or fleece, as evenings can be cool, especially in desert and high-altitude areas.

Sun Protection

- Sunscreen is a must, preferably with a high SPF to protect against the intense sun. Reapply regularly, especially if spending extended time outdoors.
- A wide-brimmed hat or cap will provide shade and protect your face and neck.
- Sunglasses with UV protection are essential for comfort and eye protection.

Hydration

A reusable water bottle is crucial to stay hydrated, especially when engaging in outdoor activities. Many places offer refill stations, making it easier to keep your water supply topped up.

Footwear

Comfortable walking shoes are a must for city explorations. Shoes should provide good support as you may walk more than usual. If you plan to hike, quality hiking boots or trail shoes are essential. They provide better grip and support on uneven terrain and protect your feet from thorns and rocks.

Visa and Entry Requirements

International travelers planning a trip to Arizona should carefully check the visa requirements, as they vary depending on the country of origin. Understanding these requirements is crucial for a smooth entry into the United States.

Visa Waiver Program (VWP)

- Travelers from countries that are part of the VWP can enter the U.S. without a visa for stays of up to 90 days. This applies to tourism, certain types of business visits, and transit purposes.
- To use the VWP, travelers must have authorization through the Electronic System for Travel Authorization (ESTA). This should be applied for at least 72 hours before travel, but it's advisable to do it as soon as travel plans are confirmed.
- ESTA is valid for two years or until the traveler's passport expires, whichever comes first, and allows for multiple entries into the U.S.

Visitors from Non-VWP Countries

- Travelers from countries not in the VWP need to obtain a visa for travel to the U.S. This typically involves an application process through a U.S. embassy or consulate in their home country.
- The type of visa required will depend on the purpose of the visit. Most tourists will apply for a B-2 tourist visa, which usually requires documentation of the travel plan and proof of financial means to cover the trip.
- The process can take time, so it's important to apply well in advance of the intended travel date.

General Entry Requirements

- A passport valid for at least six months beyond the period of intended stay is generally required.
- Visitors may also need to show proof of return or onward travel and sufficient funds to support themselves during their stay.
- Upon arrival, travelers will go through U.S. Customs and Border Protection, where they will be asked about their travel purpose and duration.
- It's important to stay updated on the visa and entry requirements, as these policies can change. Consulting the official website of the U.S. Department of State or contacting the nearest U.S. embassy or consulate will provide the most current and detailed information.

Transportation: Getting To and Around Arizona

Navigating Arizona, a state known for its vast landscapes and diverse regions, requires some planning in terms of transportation. Here's a guide to the various options available for getting to and around Arizona:

Air Travel

Phoenix Sky Harbor International Airport: This is the primary gateway to Arizona and one of the busiest airports in the United States. It serves a multitude of domestic flights and a growing number of international destinations.

Tucson International Airport: Another significant airport in Arizona, located in the southern part of the state. It offers a range of domestic flights and limited international service, making it a convenient entry point for visitors heading to southern Arizona.

Road Travel

Highways: Arizona's extensive network of highways and interstates makes road travel a popular and convenient option. Major highways such as I-10, I-17, and I-40 facilitate easy access to various parts of the state.

Car Rentals: Available at all major airports and cities, renting a car is a flexible way to explore Arizona, especially for reaching destinations that are not easily accessible by public transportation.

Shuttles and Tours: For those who prefer not to drive, there are shuttle services and guided tours available, especially to popular destinations like the Grand Canyon.

Public Transportation

Urban Areas: In larger cities like Phoenix and Tucson, public transportation systems including buses and light rail lines are available. These services are useful for navigating city centers and surrounding neighborhoods.

Limitations: Outside of major urban areas, public transportation options are significantly limited. Smaller towns and natural attractions often lack public transit, so having a car is essential for exploring these areas.

Vehicle Choice: For visiting national parks, forests, and other natural attractions, a high-clearance vehicle or even a four-wheel drive might be necessary, especially for unpaved or rugged roads.

Rental Options: Many car rental agencies offer a variety of vehicles suitable for different terrains. Ensure that you're comfortable with the vehicle size and handling, especially if planning to drive on less developed roads.

Health and Travel Insurance

Prioritizing health and safety is essential when traveling to Arizona, a state known for its adventurous outdoor activities and extreme climate variations. Here's what travelers need to know about health considerations and the importance of travel insurance:

Travel Insurance

Medical Emergencies: Choose a travel insurance policy that covers medical emergencies. Medical care in the United States can be very expensive, and having comprehensive coverage can alleviate financial stress in case of unexpected illness or injury.

Trip Cancellations: Opt for a policy that includes trip cancellation coverage. This can be invaluable if unforeseen circumstances, like severe weather or health issues, force you to cancel or cut short your trip.

Lost Luggage: Insurance that covers lost, stolen, or damaged luggage provides peace of mind, especially if you're carrying valuable items like cameras or hiking gear.

Activity Coverage: If your trip includes specific activities like hiking, mountain biking, or other adventure sports, make sure your insurance policy covers these. Some activities may be considered high risk and not covered under standard policies.

Healthcare Facilities

Urban Areas: In cities like Phoenix and Tucson, healthcare facilities are readily available, including hospitals and urgent care centers.

Remote Areas: When traveling to more remote locations, such as national parks or desert regions, be aware that healthcare facilities may be far away. Always know the location of the nearest medical facility and keep emergency contact numbers handy.

Staying Healthy in Arizona's Climate

Hydration: The dry desert climate can lead to dehydration quickly, especially during the hot summer months. Carry water with you at all times and drink regularly, even if you don't feel thirsty.

Heat-Related Illnesses: Be aware of the signs of heat exhaustion and heat stroke, which can include dizziness, headache, and nausea. Avoid outdoor activities during the hottest part of the day and take frequent breaks in the shade or indoors.

The Grand Canyon, designated as a UNESCO World Heritage Site, stands as one of the most awe-inspiring natural wonders on the planet. This majestic canyon, shaped by the relentless force of the Colorado River over millions of years, is a showcase of nature's artistry. Its vast expanse reveals a cross-section of the earth's crust, displaying an array of deep valleys, imposing cliffs, and a spectrum of geological colors and formations. The layers of rock tell a story of earth's history, some dating back as far as 1.8 billion years.

The canyon stretches across northern Arizona, offering a variety of landscapes and experiences. From the densely forested rims to the arid desert stretches below, it's a place of extreme contrasts. The South Rim, open all year, is the most accessible and hence the most visited part, providing breathtaking panoramic views and a range of visitor facilities. The North Rim, which is higher in elevation and cooler in climate, offers a more secluded experience and is open seasonally.

As you stand at the edge of this immense chasm, the views extend over rugged terrain and through layers of red, orange, and brown hues, changing color with the movement of the sun. The Grand Canyon is not just a visual spectacle; it's an invitation to explore – whether through hiking its many trails, experiencing the thrill of white-water rafting on the Colorado River, or simply taking in the beauty from one of its many overlooks.

The Grand Canyon is not only a geological wonder but also a cultural one. It has been a sacred site for Native American tribes for thousands of years, and today, it continues to hold deep spiritual significance. The canyon's history is rich and multifaceted, encompassing the stories and traditions of its native inhabitants, the explorations of European settlers, and its ongoing preservation as a national treasure.

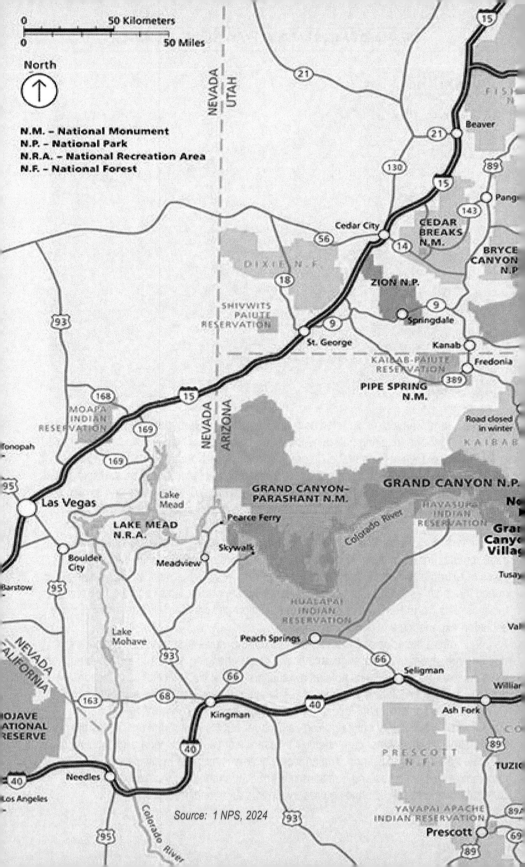

Source: 1 NPS, 2024

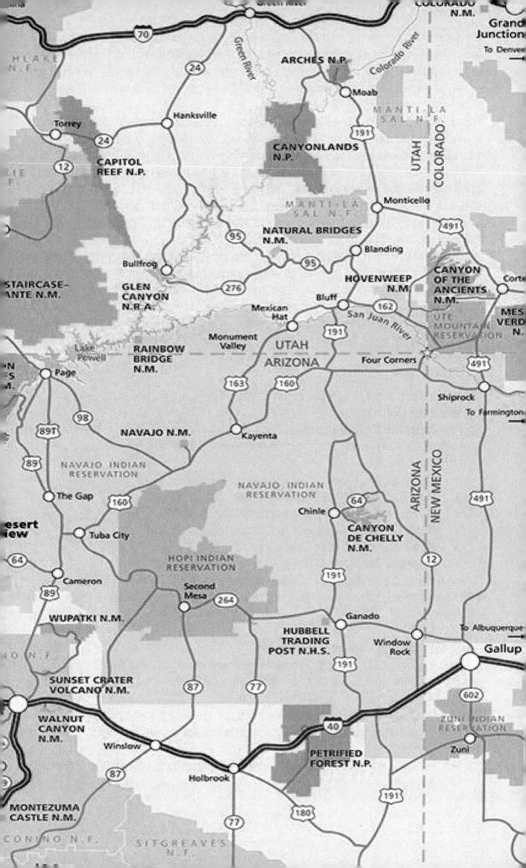

The Grand Canyon, a marvel of the natural world, is characterized by its immense size and unique geological features. Spanning 277 miles (446 kilometers) in length, the canyon varies in width, reaching up to 18 miles (29 kilometers) at its widest points. Its depth is equally impressive, plunging more than a mile (1.6 kilometers) at certain locations, revealing a complex layering of rock strata.

This colossal chasm is primarily divided into two main sections accessible to visitors: the South Rim and the North Rim. These rims, delineating the edges of the canyon, offer distinctly different experiences due to their varying elevations, climate, and viewpoints. The South Rim, sitting at an elevation of about 7,000 feet (2,134 meters), is renowned for its accessibility and panoramic vistas. This rim is the most visited part of the canyon due to its numerous overlooks, visitor services, and the iconic Grand Canyon Village. The viewpoints here, such as Mather Point and Yavapai Observation Station, provide some of the most photographed scenes of the canyon.

In contrast, the North Rim, at an elevation of around 8,000 feet (2,438 meters), presents a quieter and more secluded experience. It's characterized by a cooler climate, lush vegetation, and fewer crowds. The views from the North Rim, such as those from Point Imperial and Cape Royal, offer a different perspective of the canyon's majesty. The higher elevation results in a more diverse array of plant and animal life, adding to the unique experience of this rim.

Entrance Pass Information for Visitors

All guests are required to possess a valid entrance pass to gain access to the park.

Explore Pass Options

Special Days with No Entrance Fee: On specific days, the park waives its entrance fees to encourage visitors to explore and celebrate significant national days. These days include:

- **Martin Luther King, Jr. Day:** January 15
- **First Day of National Park Week:** April 20
- **Juneteenth National Independence Day:** June 19
- **Great American Outdoors Act Anniversary:** August 4
- **National Public Lands Day:** September 28
- **Veterans Day:** November 11

Please note, on these special days, while the entrance fee is waived, other charges such as for reservations, camping, lodging, and tours remain applicable unless explicitly stated otherwise.

Admission for Non-Commercial Groups

Non-commercial groups visiting the park include various organizations such as church groups, college/school clubs, youth organizations like Girl Scouts and Boy Scouts, and service organizations.

Fees for non-commercial groups are determined by the vehicle's capacity:

- Vehicles designed to hold 16 or fewer individuals are subject to a $35.00 vehicle permit.
- For vehicles designed to carry more than 16 individuals, an $8.00 per person fee is applied.

Guide to Selecting the Right Pass for Grand Canyon National Park
This guide is designed to help you choose the appropriate pass based on your specific circumstances and ensure a smooth visit to the Grand Canyon National Park.

1. Access Pass for US Residents with Permanent Disabilities
Cost: Free, Lifetime validity
Eligibility: US citizens or permanent residents with documented permanent disabilities.
Benefits: Grants access to over 2,000 federal recreation sites. May offer discounts on certain fees such as such as camping, boat launching, swimming, etc.
Important: Must be obtained in person with proof of disability and residency. Digital copies not accepted. Non-transferable.

2. Military Passes for Service Members and Families
Active-Duty Pass: Free, valid through the end of the next calendar year. For current US military and dependents.
Military Lifetime Pass: Free, lifetime validity. For Gold Star Families and US military veterans.
Benefits: Access to over 2,000 federal recreation areas. Non-transferable, requires proof of eligibility.
Scan for more Info:

https://www.nps.gov/planyourvisit/veterans-and-gold-star-families-free-access.htm

3. 4th Grade Pass for Families with a 4th Grader
Cost: Free, valid for the school year and the following summer.
Eligibility: US 4th graders with a paper voucher from the Every Kid Outdoors website.
Benefits: Admits pass holder and passengers in a private vehicle.
Note: Voucher must be printed; digital versions not accepted.
https://www.everykidoutdoors.gov/index.htm

4. Senior Passes for US Residents Aged 62+
Lifetime Pass: $80 | **Annual Pass:** $20
Benefits: Access to over 2,000 federal recreation sites, potential discounts on amenity fees. Pass is non-transferable and requires proof of age and residency.
Details: https://www.nps.gov/planyourvisit/senior-pass-changes.htm

5. Interagency Annual Pass (America the Beautiful Pass)
Cost: $80 annual pass
Eligibility: Open to all.
Benefits: Access to over 2,000 federal recreation areas for one year from the month of purchase. Pass is shared between two owners but non-transferable to others.

6. Grand Canyon National Park Annual Pass
Cost: $70 annual pass
Benefits: Unlimited access to Grand Canyon National Park for one year. Admits all passengers in a single vehicle or the pass holder and their immediate family.
Purchase: Available in-person at Grand Canyon entrance stations.

7. Standard Entrance Fees

Private Vehicle: $35 (valid for 7 days, includes all passengers)
Motorcycle: $30
Per Person: $20 (for bicyclists, hikers, pedestrians)
Note: Entrance fees are valid for both South and North Rim visits. Cash not accepted, credit/debit only.

Where to Purchase Your Pass

- Online, prior to arrival.
- In-person upon arrival (card only) at Grand Canyon entrance stations or automated fee machines.

Operating Hours and Seasonal Information

South Rim - South Entrance

Open: 24/7
Details: Both the Desert View (East Entrance) and South Entrance are accessible around the clock, every day. Payment options include credit cards, Recreation.gov, Your Pass Now, and America the Beautiful passes; cash is currently not accepted. The South Entrance, near Tusayan, Arizona, experiences high traffic volumes, with potential wait times up to 2 hours between 9:30 am and 4 pm. The East Entrance at Desert View generally has shorter wait times.
Holidays 2024–2025 (South Rim): Open 24 hours on all listed holidays, including New Year's Day, Martin Luther King, Jr. Day, Washington's Birthday, Memorial Day, Juneteenth National Independence Day, Independence Day, Labor Day, Columbus Day, Veterans Day, Thanksgiving Day, and Christmas Day.

North Rim

Season: The North Rim operates seasonally, open from May 15, 2024, with lodging and campground reservations recommended. Note the elevation over 8000 feet/2438 m, which may affect those with respiratory or heart conditions. The North Rim is closed to all vehicles from December 1st to May 14th, with no visitor services available.
Holidays 2024–2025 (North Rim): Closed on New Year's Day, Martin Luther King, Jr. Day, Washington's Birthday, and Christmas Day. Open 24 hours on Memorial Day, Juneteenth National Independence Day, Independence Day, Labor Day, and Columbus Day. Open from sunrise to sunset on Veterans Day and Thanksgiving Day.
November Day Use (North Rim): From November 1 to November 30, the North Rim is open for day use from sunrise to sunset. Lodging and campground are closed during this period.

Desert View (East Entrance - South Rim)

Open: 24/7
Details: Accessible all day, every day, offering visitors spectacular views of the Grand Canyon and the Colorado River. Desert View services are generally open to visitors. The Desert View Campground operates seasonally.
Holidays 2024–2025 (Desert View): Open 24 hours on all listed holidays.

General Note: Visitors should plan their trip keeping in mind the seasonal operations, especially when intending to visit the North Rim. Always check the latest information for any updates or changes to park operations and seasonal exceptions.

South Rim of Grand Canyon

The South Rim of the Grand Canyon, renowned for its exceptional accessibility, welcomes visitors throughout the year, making it the most frequented section of the canyon. This accessibility is one of its key attractions, allowing a vast number of visitors, regardless of the season, to experience the grandeur of the canyon.

This rim's popularity is further enhanced by the extensive range of facilities and services available to tourists. From ample parking areas and well-developed viewpoints to a variety of dining and lodging options, the South Rim is well-equipped to cater to the needs of its visitors. The Grand Canyon Village, located here, serves as a central hub, providing not only accommodations and food services but also educational exhibits, shops, and cultural demonstrations.

The South Rim's network of trails and viewpoints is another aspect that contributes to its appeal. Trails like the Rim Trail offer relatively easy walking paths along the edge of the canyon, providing spectacular and ever-changing views. More adventurous visitors can embark on the Bright Angel or South Kaibab trails, which descend into the depths of the canyon for a more immersive experience.

Moreover, the South Rim is well-connected in terms of transportation. The Grand Canyon Railway, which runs from Williams, Arizona, to the South Rim, offers a unique and scenic way to reach the canyon. Additionally, shuttle bus services within the park make it convenient for visitors to travel between various points of interest without the hassle of driving and parking.

South Rim Grand Canyon Park Free Shuttle Bus Service

Shuttle Bus Service Overview The shuttle buses on the Village, Kaibab/Rim, and Hermits Rest Routes operate every 10 to 15 minutes throughout the daytime. Starting an hour before sunrise until an hour after sunset, the frequency shifts to approximately every 30 minutes. The Tusayan Route offers service every 20 minutes, beginning at 8 am from the IMAX Theater and concluding at 9:45 pm.

Guidelines for Shuttle Use

- Consuming food or having open drink containers on the bus is not permitted.
- Pets are not allowed, with the exception of ADA-certified service animals.
- The buses are designed to accommodate wheelchairs up to 30 inches (76 cm) in width and 48 inches (121 cm) in length. Wheelchairs exceeding these dimensions cannot be accommodated.
- Strollers must be folded before boarding. The shuttle cannot accommodate oversized or jogging strollers. If using a baby-back carrier, please remove it while seated.
- Each shuttle can carry two to three bicycles. However, bicycles with tag-alongs, baby trailers, or wheels smaller than 16 inches (41 cm) cannot be accommodated. Bicycle riders are responsible for loading and unloading their bicycles.
- Shuttles will only stop at designated shuttle stops, ensuring a smooth and efficient travel experience for all passengers.

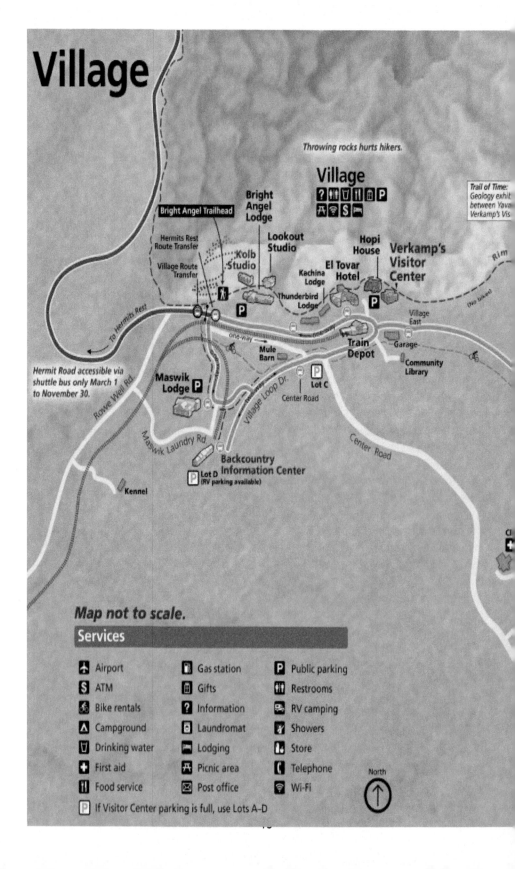

Village

Throwing rocks hurts hikers.

Village

Bright Angel Trailhead

Hermits Rest Route Transfer

Village Route Transfer

Bright Angel Lodge

Lookout Studio

Kolb Studio

Kachina Lodge

Thunderbird Lodge

Hopi House

El Tovar Hotel

Verkamp's Visitor Center

Trail of Time: Geology exhibit between Yava Verkamp's Vis

Rim

Village East

To Hermits Rest

Hermit Road accessible via shuttle bus only March 1 to November 30.

Rowe Well Rd

Maswik Lodge

Mule Barn

Village Loop Dr.

Lot C

Center Road

Train Depot

Garage

Community Library

Center Road

Maswik Laundry Rd.

Backcountry Information Center

Lot D (RV parking available)

Kennel

Map not to scale.

Services

✈ Airport	🛢 Gas station	P Public parking
S ATM	🎁 Gifts	🚻 Restrooms
🚲 Bike rentals	❓ Information	🚐 RV camping
▲ Campground	🧺 Laundromat	🚿 Showers
🚰 Drinking water	🛏 Lodging	🏪 Store
➕ First aid	🌳 Picnic area	📞 Telephone
🍴 Food service	✉ Post office	📶 Wi-Fi
P If Visitor Center parking is full, use Lots A–D		

North

↑

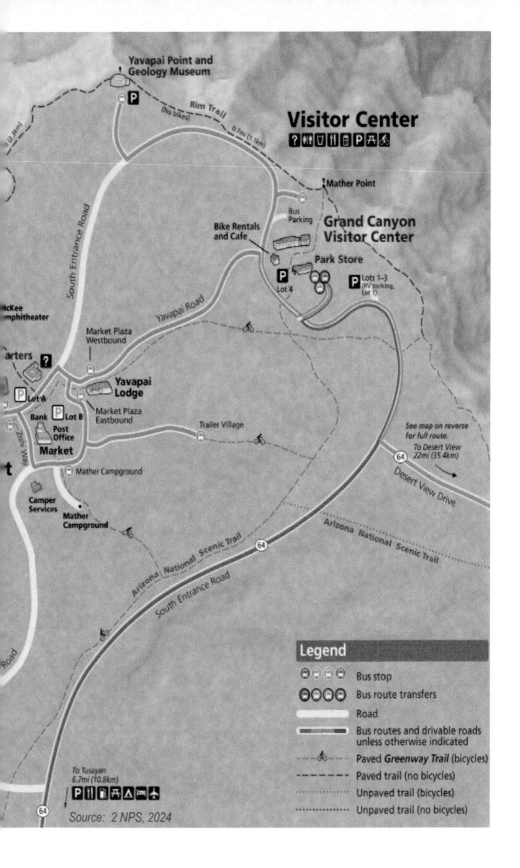

Yavapai Point and Geology Museum

Rim Trail
(No bikes)
0.7mi (1.1km)

Visitor Center

Mather Point

Bus Parking

Bike Rentals and Cafe

Grand Canyon Visitor Center

Park Store

Lot 4

Lots 1–3
(RV parking, Lot 1)

South Entrance Road

McKee Amphitheater

Yavapai Road

Market Plaza Westbound

Headquarters

Lot A

Yavapai Lodge

Market Plaza Eastbound

Trailer Village

Bank   Lot B

Post Office

Market

Mather Campground

Camper Services

Mather Campground

Arizona National Scenic Trail

See map on reverse for full route.
To Desert View
22mi (35.4km)

Desert View Drive

Arizona National Scenic Trail

64

South Entrance Road

Arizona National Scenic Trail

To Tusayan
6.7mi (10.8km)

Source: 2 NPS, 2024

Legend

⊖⊖⊖⊖	Bus stop
⊖⊖⊖⊖	Bus route transfers
▬▬▬	Road
▬▬▬	Bus routes and drivable roads unless otherwise indicated
– ⬲ –	Paved *Greenway Trail* (bicycles)
– – –	Paved trail (no bicycles)
·······	Unpaved trail (bicycles)
·······	Unpaved trail (no bicycles)

Overview of South Rim Trail by Distance

The South Rim Trail offers a comprehensive and scenic journey along the edge of the Grand Canyon, with a total length of 12.8 miles (20.6 km). (*Pet friendly*)

1. South Kaibab Trailhead to Pipe Creek Vista: 0.9 mi (1.4 km)
2. Pipe Creek Vista to Mather Point: 1.4 mi (2.3 km)
3. Mather Point to Yavapai Point: 0.7 mi (1.1 km)
4. Yavapai Point (Trail of Time) to Verkamp's: 1.4 mi (2.3 km)
5. Verkamp's to Bright Angel Trailhead: 0.5 mi (0.8 km)
6. Bright Angel Trailhead to Trailview Overlook: 0.5 mi (0.8 km)
7. Trailview Overlook to Maricopa Point: 0.7 mi (1.1 km)
8. Maricopa Point to Powell Point: 0.5 mi (0.8 km)
9. Powell Point to Hopi Point: 0.3 mi (0.5 km)
10. Hopi Point to Mohave Point: 1.0 mi (1.6 km)
11. Mohave Point to The Abyss: 1.1 mi (1.8 km)
12. The Abyss to Monument Creek Vista: 1.0 mi (1.6 km)
13. Monument Creek Vista to Pima Point: 1.8 mi (2.9 km)
14. Pima Point to Hermits Rest: 1.0 mi (1.6 km)

Total distance: 12.8 mi (20.6 km)

Overview of the Greenway Trail by Distance

These trails are friendly for hiking, biking, and leashed pets.

- **South Kaibab Trailhead to Pipe Creek Vista:** 0.9 mi (1.4 km)
- **Pipe Creek Vista to Grand Canyon Visitor Center:** 1.5 mi (2.4 km)
- **Grand Canyon Visitor Center to Market Plaza:** 0.9 mi (1.4 km)
- **Market Plaza to Village:** 1.0 mi (1.6 km)
- **Village to Hermit Road:** 0.6 mi (1.0 km)
- **Monument Creek Vista to Pima Point:** 1.8 mi (2.9 km)
- **Grand Canyon Visitor Center to Trailer Village:** 0.7 mi (1.2 km)
- **Grand Canyon Visitor Center to Mather Campground:** 1.2 mi (2.0 km)
- **Grand Canyon Visitor Center to Tusayan:** 6.6 mi (10.6 km)

Road Trails by Distance

Here's a consolidated and mixed format for the road trails in and around the Grand Canyon Visitor Center and Village, suitable for those looking to explore the area:

From Grand Canyon Visitor Center to:

- Desert View: 22.0 mi (35.4 km)
- Market Plaza: 0.9 mi (1.4 km)
- Tusayan: 6.7 mi (10.8 km)
- Village: 2.1 mi (3.4 km)

From Village to:

- Grand Canyon Visitor Center: 2.1 mi (3.4 km)
- Hermits Rest: 7.4 mi (11.9 km)
- Market Plaza: 1.4 mi (2.3 km)
- Tusayan: 6.3 mi (10.1 km)

Popular South Rim Viewpoints and Attractions: There are several attractions along the South Rim of the Grand Canyon that provide visitors with different perspectives of the canyon's vastness and beauty. Among these, several stand out as must-visit locations.

Mather Point

Mather Point is often the first view of the canyon for many visitors, owing to its proximity to the Grand Canyon Visitor Center. This viewpoint offers a dramatic introduction to the grandeur of the canyon, with expansive views of the vast chasm, the Colorado River, and the Phantom Ranch area. The railing-protected overlook gives an unobstructed view, making it a popular spot for both sunrise and sunset viewings.

Yavapai Observation Station

Yavapai Observation Station provides a unique vantage point with its large, glass-paneled observation windows that allow for unimpeded viewing of the canyon. Located slightly east of Mather Point, this station also features geological exhibits and telescopes for a closer look at the canyon's features. The panoramic views from Yavapai encompass several key landmarks of the Grand Canyon, including the Bright Angel Trail and the Colorado River.

Rim Trail

The Rim Trail is a scenic walking path that stretches along the edge of the canyon, offering continually changing views and perspectives. This relatively flat trail runs for about 13 miles (21 kilometers) along the rim, allowing visitors to walk as little or as much as they like. The trail provides numerous photo opportunities and spots to simply sit and absorb the awe-inspiring landscape.

Bright Angel Trail: The Bright Angel Trail, renowned for its popularity among hikers venturing into the Grand Canyon, offers a mix of challenge and reward. This trail takes you deep into the canyon, where you're treated to extraordinary vistas and a close-up look at the canyon's geological wonders. Along the path, hikers will find rest houses and water stations, though it's crucial to come prepared for a demanding trek. Hiking without a backcountry permit is not allowed.

Trail Essentials:

Terrain: The trail is a well-maintained dirt path, steep and clearly marked, with occasional shade provided by the towering canyon walls, varying with the day's time. In winter or early spring, the upper trail sections can become notably icy.

Elevation at Start: The journey begins at 6,850 feet, west of Bright Angel Lodge near the mule corral on the South Rim.

Water and Rest: Water stations and rest houses dot the trail, with year-round water availability at the trailhead and Indian Garden, and seasonal water along the trail. Note: Water availability is subject to change due to pipeline maintenance; always check current conditions at the Visitor Center or Backcountry Information Center.

Safety: Park rangers patrol the trail randomly. A Ranger Station at Indian Garden offers assistance and information.

Hiking Advice:

- The trail offers captivating views that can distract from the actual distance covered. Its deceiving steepness on the descent means the return climb may take twice as long.
- Carrying sufficient water is crucial, despite water stations along the path. Each hiker should have their own supply, and group hiking necessitates individual water for each member.
- Eating and staying hydrated is essential; hiking in the canyon demands considerable energy.

Mules on the Trail: Recent encounters between hikers and mules have led to serious incidents. For everyone's safety:

- Step to the uphill side of the trail, away from edges, when mules approach.
- Follow the wrangler's instructions, remaining silent and still until the last mule has passed by at least 50 feet (15 meters).

Important Caution: Attempting a day trip from the rim to the river and back, especially from May to September, is strongly discouraged due to the intense physical demand and potential for extreme heat exposure.

Trailhead Directions: Located on the South Rim, the trail starts just west of Bright Angel Lodge, initiated by a path that runs along the rim, beginning by the mule corral.

Yielding on the Trail: Giving way to uphill hikers is a courtesy that ensures safety and respect for all trail users, helping maintain a smooth flow on the path.

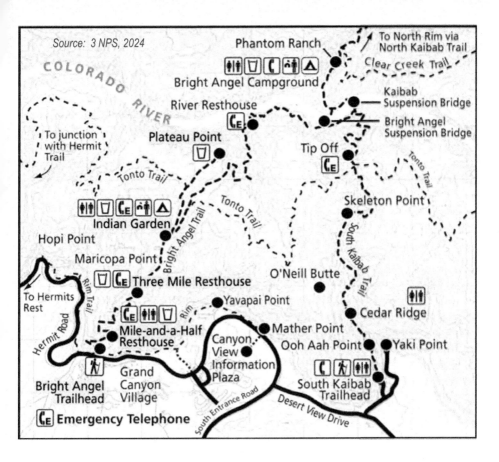

Source: 3 NPS, 2024

COLORADO RIVER

Phantom Ranch

To North Rim via
North Kaibab Trail

Clear Creek Trail

Bright Angel Campground

River Resthouse

Kaibab
Suspension Bridge

Bright Angel
Suspension Bridge

To junction
with Hermit
Trail

Plateau Point

Tip Off

Tonto Trail

Skeleton Point

Indian Garden

Hopi Point

Maricopa Point

Three Mile Resthouse

O'Neill Butte

To Hermits
Rest

Yavapai Point

Cedar Ridge

Mile-and-a-Half
Resthouse

Mather Point

Ooh Aah Point

Yaki Point

Canyon
View
Information
Plaza

Grand
Canyon
Village

Bright Angel
Trailhead

South Kaibab
Trailhead

South Entrance Road

Desert View Drive

Emergency Telephone

Grand Canyon Railway

Grand Canyon Railway: For a unique and historical approach to the canyon, the Grand Canyon Railway offers a memorable journey from Williams, Arizona, to the South Rim. The train ride includes entertainment, historical anecdotes, and stunning scenery, making it an enjoyable experience for all ages.

Desert View Drive: This scenic route stretches for 25 miles along the rim from Grand Canyon Village to the Desert View Watchtower. The drive offers numerous pullouts and viewpoints, including Moran Point and Navajo Point, each offering distinct views of the canyon.

Desert View Watchtower: Designed by architect Mary Colter, this 70-foot high stone tower at the eastern end of the South Rim provides one of the widest views of the Grand Canyon. The tower's interior walls feature murals by Hopi artist Fred Kabotie, showcasing the cultural significance of the area.

Hermit Road: Accessible by shuttle bus, bicycle, or on foot (private vehicles are restricted for most of the year), this route offers some of the most dramatic views of the canyon. There are several overlooks along the way, including Hopi Point, one of the best spots for sunset views.

Market Plaza: This is the central area for services on the South Rim, featuring a general store, post office, bank, and other amenities. It's a convenient stop for visitors to stock up on supplies or take a break from exploring.

Kolb Studio: Perched on the rim of the canyon, this historic studio and residence now houses an art gallery and a bookstore. It was once the home and business of the Kolb brothers, pioneer photographers at the Grand Canyon.

Geological Museum: Located at Yavapai Point, this museum provides educational exhibits about the geological history of the Grand Canyon, including how it was formed. The museum's large windows also offer a spectacular view of the canyon.

North Rim of Grand Canyon

The North Rim of the Grand Canyon presents a distinctly different experience compared to its more frequented counterpart, the South Rim. Open seasonally from mid-May to mid-October, the North Rim offers visitors a chance to explore the canyon in a more secluded and intimate setting. This limited seasonality is due to the higher elevation of the North Rim, which sits at about 8,000 feet, leading to heavier snowfall and colder temperatures during the winter months.

The tranquility of the North Rim is one of its most appealing features. With fewer visitors, it provides a more serene atmosphere, allowing for a more personal connection with the natural surroundings. The landscape here is also more varied and lusher, with a higher proportion of green meadows and dense forests of aspen and pine, contrasting with the more arid environment of the South Rim.

During its open season, the North Rim offers a variety of outdoor activities and experiences. Hiking trails, such as the North Kaibab Trail, provide dramatic views and access to different parts of the canyon. Point Imperial and Cape Royal are among the most popular viewpoints, offering spectacular vistas of the canyon and the Colorado River. The relative solitude of the North Rim also makes it ideal for wildlife viewing, with a higher likelihood of encountering wildlife such as deer, turkeys, and a variety of bird species.

For visitors planning to stay overnight, the North Rim has lodging options including the historic Grand Canyon Lodge, which offers a rustic experience with its cabin accommodations. There are also several campgrounds in the area, providing a perfect opportunity for those looking to immerse themselves in the natural beauty of the Grand Canyon.

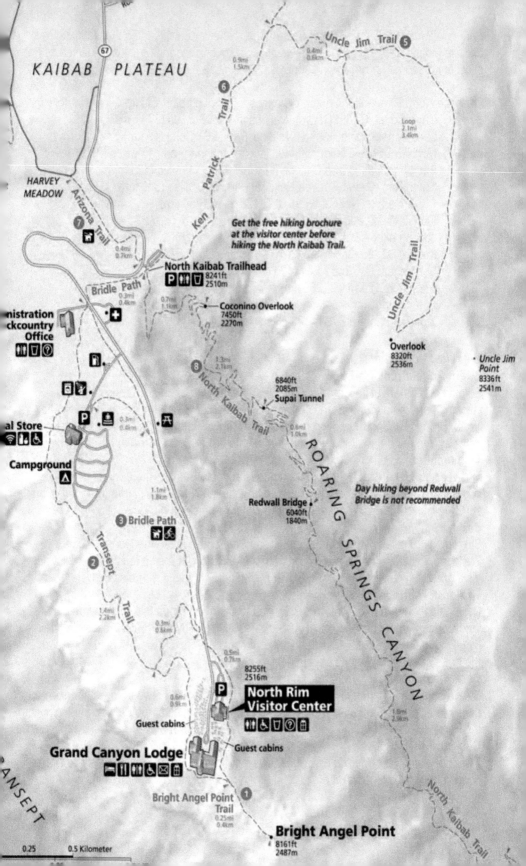

KAIBAB PLATEAU

67

Uncle Jim Trail 5

0.9mi 1.5km

0.4mi 0.6km

6

Loop 2.1mi 3.4km

HARVEY MEADOW

Arizona Trail

7

0.4mi 0.7km

Ken Patrick Trail

Get the free hiking brochure at the visitor center before hiking the North Kaibab Trail.

Uncle Jim Trail

North Kaibab Trailhead
8241ft
2510m

0.3mi
0.4km

Bridle Path

0.7mi
1.1km

Coconino Overlook
7450ft
2270m

Overlook
8320ft
2536m

Uncle Jim Point
8336ft
2541m

nistration
ckcountry
Office

North Kaibab Trail

8

1.3mi
2.1km

6840ft
2085m
Supai Tunnel

al Store

P

0.3mi
0.4km

0.6mi
1.0km

ROARING SPRINGS CANYON

Campground

Day hiking beyond Redwall Bridge is not recommended

1.1mi
1.8km

3 Bridle Path

Redwall Bridge
6040ft
1840m

Transept Trail

2

1.4mi
2.2km

0.3mi
0.5km

0.5mi
0.7km

8255ft
2516m

P

North Rim
Visitor Center

0.6mi
0.9km

1.8mi
2.9km

Guest cabins

Grand Canyon Lodge

Guest cabins

North Kaibab Trail

TRANSEPT

Bright Angel Point
Trail

1

0.25mi
0.4km

Bright Angel Point
8161ft
2487m

0.25   0.5 Kilometer

Source of Map: NPS, 2024. For further details, consider downloading the National Park Service Mobile App https://www.nps.gov/grca/planyourvisit/app.htm, which serves as an excellent resource for organizing your visit.

From the North Rim Visitor Center, distances to various points of interest are as follows:
- Cape Royal, Grand Canyon National Park: 23 miles (37 km)
- Lees Ferry, Grand Canyon National Park: 90 miles (145 km)
- North Entrance Station, Grand Canyon National Park: 13 miles (21 km)
- Point Imperial, Grand Canyon National Park: 11 miles (18 km)
- South Rim, Grand Canyon National Park: 210 miles (338 km)
- Bryce Canyon National Park, UT: 158 miles (254 km)
- Flagstaff, AZ: 208 miles (335 km)
- Jacob Lake, AZ: 44 miles (71 km)
- Kanab, UT: 80 miles (129 km)
- Las Vegas, NV: 266 miles (428 km)
- Page, AZ: 124 miles (200 km)
- Pipe Spring National Monument, UT: 87 miles (140 km)
- Zion National Park, UT: 122 miles (196 km)

Overview North Rim Day Hikes
Bright Angel Point Trail
Embark on a brief yet invigorating 0.5-mile (0.8 km) journey to experience an awe-inspiring panorama of the Grand Canyon. Starting from either the log shelter near the North Rim Visitor Center parking or the Grand Canyon Lodge's rear porch, this paved pathway demands about 30 minutes of your time but rewards you with breathtaking views.
Transept Trail
This 2-mile (3.2 km) trek, perfect for an hour's adventure, skirts the edge of the canyon from the Grand Canyon Lodge to the area beyond the North Rim Campground. It offers stunning vistas along The Transept, a captivating side canyon.
Bridle Path
Stretching 1.9 miles (3.1 km) from the Grand Canyon Lodge to the North Kaibab Trailhead, this path parallels the road and welcomes both pets on leashes and bicycles. It's a great way to spend an hour, exploring the area on this well-maintained trail.
Widforss Trail
Delve into the heart of nature on a 9.6-mile (15.5 km) roundtrip that blends forest landscapes with canyon views. Allot six hours to fully enjoy this route. Access the trailhead by taking a dirt road 0.25 miles (0.4 km) south of Cape Royal Road. A guide brochure at the trail's start enhances the experience.
Cape Final Trail
Set off on a 4.2-mile (6.8 km) roundtrip journey, taking roughly two to three hours, through dense forests to Cape Final. The trail unveils stunning vistas of the canyon stretching into the Painted Desert. Starting point is 2.4 miles (3.9 km) north of Cape Royal's parking area.
Cliff Spring Trail
This 0.8-mile (1.3 km) return hike, ideal for an hour's exploration, winds down to a forested ravine ending at a significant boulder under an overhang with a spring on its cliffside

water not recommended for drinking). The trailhead is just across from a pullout along a curve 0.3 miles (0.5 km) north of Cape Royal.

Cape Royal Trail

Enjoy a leisurely 0.8-mile (1.3 km) stroll, requiring about an hour, on a flat, paved path offering scenic views of the canyon, Angels Window, and the Colorado River, complete with educational signage about the natural history of the area. The trail starts on the southeast side of Cape Royal's parking lot.

Uncle Jim Trail

A 4.7-mile (7.6 km) roundtrip hike that takes you through dense forests to a viewpoint over the canyon and the North Kaibab Trail switchbacks, taking approximately three hours. The journey begins at the North Kaibab Trail parking lot. Be prepared to encounter mules and follow the wrangler's instructions.

Ken Patrick Trail

Covering 9.8 miles (15.8 km) from Point Imperial to the North Kaibab Trail parking area, this six-hour, one-way hike offers a passage through dense forests and along the rim on an unmaintained path.

North Kaibab Trail

Offering various distances and durations, this trail is the primary path from the North Rim down into the canyon. Trail conditions can vary, and attempting a round trip to the Colorado River in a single day is highly discouraged. Mule trains frequent this path, so hikers should be prepared to step aside and follow any instructions given.

Arizona Trail

A 12.1-mile (19.5 km) section of this trail passes through the park, starting near the north entrance and running parallel to AZ 67 up to its junction with the North Kaibab Trail, taking about seven hours. This route is accessible to both pets on leashes and bicycles, offering a unique way to experience the park's natural beauty.

Popular North Rim Viewpoints and Attractions: Notable spots include Point Imperial, the highest point in the park, and Cape Royal, offering wide panoramic views. At the North Rim of the Grand Canyon, the viewpoints and attractions are characterized by their stunning vistas and serene beauty, providing visitors with a different perspective of the canyon's vastness. Among these, Point Imperial and Cape Royal stand out as must-visit locations.

Point Imperial
___

Point Imperial, the highest point in the Grand Canyon National Park, reaches an elevation of 8,803 feet. This lofty vantage point offers visitors a unique view of the canyon, showcasing the narrowest and deepest part. From here, one can see the Painted Desert and the eastern end of the Grand Canyon, with layers of red and black Precambrian rocks at the bottom – some of the oldest visible rocks in the park. The viewpoint is accessible via a scenic drive that offers additional opportunities to appreciate the surrounding landscape.

A quieter viewpoint offering a beautiful perspective of the canyon. This spot is ideal for visitors seeking solitude and a place to contemplate the natural beauty around them.

Named in honor of Theodore Roosevelt 26th president of the United States for his efforts towards the preservation of Grand Canyon.
"Leave it as it is. You cannot improve on it. The ages have been at work on it, and man can only mar it. What you can do is to keep it for your children, your children's children, and for all who come after you, as the one great sight which every American...should see."

Theodore Roosevelt, Grand Canyon 1903

ROOSEVELT POINT

Named in honor of Theodore Roosevelt
26th president of the United States
for his efforts towards the preservation of Grand Canyon

"Leave it as it is. You cannot improve on it. The ages have been at work on it, and man can only mar it. What you can do is to keep it for your children, your children's children, and for all who come after you, as the one great sight which every American...should see."

Theodore Roosevelt
Grand Canyon 1903

The plateau offers a mix of geological and historical wonders. Angel's Window, a natural arch on the plateau, frames a dramatic view of the canyon below. Nearby are the ancient ruins of the Walhalla Glades Pueblo, showcasing the region's rich cultural history.

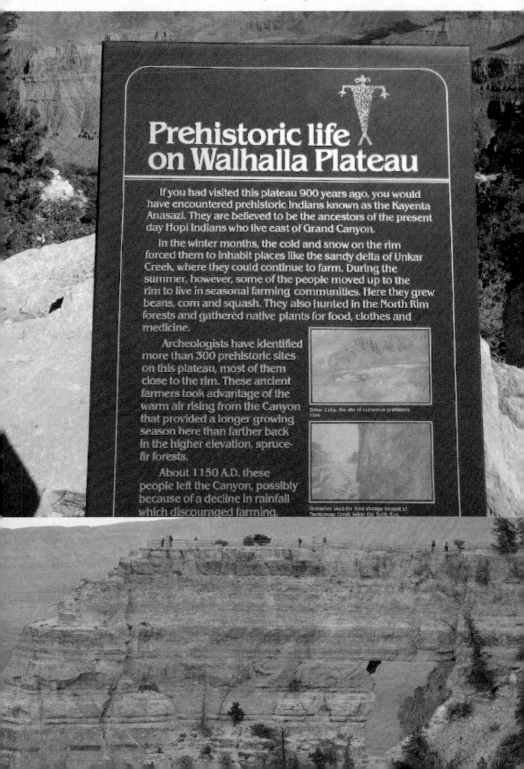

Prehistoric life on Walhalla Plateau

If you had visited this plateau 900 years ago, you would have encountered prehistoric Indians known as the Kayenta Anasazi. They are believed to be the ancestors of the present day Hopi Indians who live east of Grand Canyon.

In the winter months, the cold and snow on the rim forced them to inhabit places like the sandy delta of Unkar Creek, where they could continue to farm. During the summer, however, some of the people moved up to the rim to live in seasonal farming communities. Here they grew beans, corn and squash. They also hunted in the North Rim forests and gathered native plants for food, clothes and medicine.

Archeologists have identified more than 300 prehistoric sites on this plateau, most of them close to the rim. These ancient farmers took advantage of the warm air rising from the Canyon that provided a longer growing season here than farther back in the higher elevation, spruce-fir forests.

About 1150 A.D. these people left the Canyon, possibly because of a decline in rainfall which discouraged farming.

Unkar Delta, the site of numerous prehistoric sites.

Granaries used for food storage located at Nankoweap Creek below the North Rim.

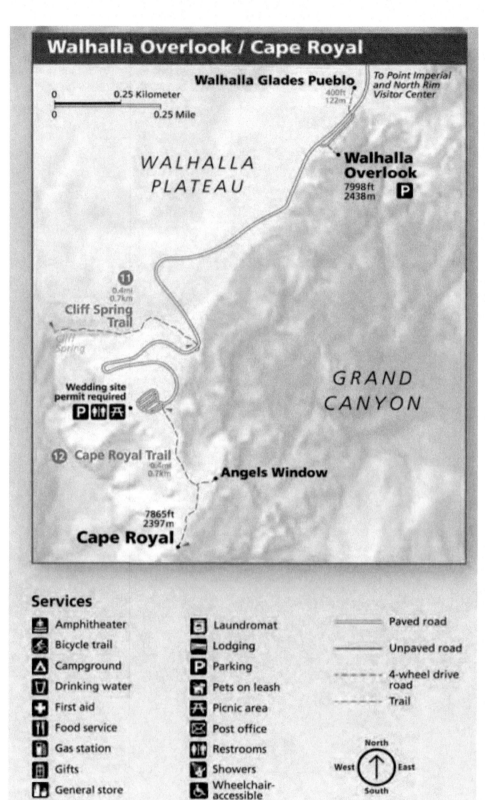

Walhalla Overlook / Cape Royal

Walhalla Glades Pueblo

To Point Imperial and North Rim Visitor Center

0   0.25 Kilometer
0   0.25 Mile

400ft
122m

WALHALLA PLATEAU

Walhalla Overlook
7998ft
2438m
P

⑪
0.4mi
0.7km

Cliff Spring Trail

Cliff Spring

GRAND CANYON

Wedding site permit required
P 🚻 ⛱

⑫ Cape Royal Trail
0.4mi
0.7km

Angels Window

7865ft
2397m

Cape Royal

Services

🔊 Amphitheater	🧺 Laundromat	═══ Paved road
🚴 Bicycle trail	🛏 Lodging	─── Unpaved road
⛺ Campground	P Parking	▬ ▬ ▬ 4-wheel drive road
💧 Drinking water	🐾 Pets on leash	— · — · — Trail
➕ First aid	⛱ Picnic area	
🍴 Food service	✉ Post office	
⛽ Gas station	🚻 Restrooms	North
🎁 Gifts	🚿 Showers	West ↑ East
🏪 General store	♿ Wheelchair-accessible	South
ℹ Information	📶 Wi-Fi	

Point Sublime Trail: Accessible via a rough dirt road, Point Sublime is one of the most remote and stunning viewpoints on the North Rim. The journey to get there is an adventure in itself and rewards visitors with panoramic views of the Grand Canyon.
Cape Final Trail: This trail offers a peaceful hike leading to impressive views of the canyon. It's less crowded, making it a good choice for those looking for a quieter experience.
Widforss Trail: A less frequented trail that combines forested beauty with canyon vistas. This hike provides a unique opportunity to enjoy both the tranquility of the forest and the awe-inspiring views of the canyon.
Star Gazing: Due to its remote location, the North Rim is an excellent place for stargazing, with clear, dark skies ideal for observing stars and constellations.

Other Attractions in and Around Grand Canyon

Black Bridge

Location: Black Bridge is located within the Grand Canyon National Park, spanning the Colorado River and accessible via the South Kaibab Trail.
Description: Black Bridge is a pedestrian-only bridge that offers visitors a unique and memorable vantage point to admire the Colorado River and the surrounding canyon scenery. It provides a spectacular perspective of the grandeur of the Grand Canyon, allowing for breathtaking photo opportunities and moments of contemplation.

Cedar Ridge

Location: Cedar Ridge is located on the South Kaibab Trail, within the Grand Canyon National Park.
Description: Cedar Ridge offers a popular hiking destination with pristine trails and stunning canyon views. This mid-point stop on the South Kaibab Trail provides a rewarding hiking experience amidst the clean and well-maintained surroundings of the Grand Canyon.
Activities: Hiking, photography, picnicking, and scenic viewing. It's a great spot for taking in the vastness of the canyon and capturing memorable photographs.

Desert View Watchtower

Location: Located at the East Entrance of the Grand Canyon National Park, near the South Rim.
Description: The Desert View Watchtower is a 7-story tower designed by noted architect Mary Colter. It offers breathtaking views of the Grand Canyon that are distinct from those seen from the main visitor center. The tower provides a unique perspective of the canyon's beauty, enriched by the cultural and historical exhibits within.

Garden Creek

Location: Within the Grand Canyon National Park, accessible via the Bright Angel Trail.
Description: Garden Creek offers a serene area within the Grand Canyon, providing a peaceful respite amidst the stunning natural beauty of the landscape. This spot is perfect for those seeking a moment of tranquility away from the busier viewpoints and trails.

Grand Canyon Museum Collection

Location: Located at 2 Albright Ave, within the Grand Canyon National Park.
Description: The Grand Canyon Museum Collection is a history museum that offers insights into the cultural and natural history of the Grand Canyon. Visitors can explore exhibits such as the unique "buckets of paint" display, which showcases the canyon's geological layers and the diversity of its natural environment.

Grand Canyon National Park - Kolb Studio

Location: Situated along Village Loop Drive, at the canyon's edge within the Grand Canyon National Park.
Description: The Kolb Studio is a historic bookstore and gallery offering visitors a chance to explore a selection of books and artwork inspired by the Grand Canyon. The studio, originally the home and business of pioneering photographers the Kolb Brothers, combines cultural history with stunning views.

Grandview Lookout Tower

Location: Positioned at 100 Coconino Rim Rd, near Grandview Point in the Grand Canyon National Park.
Description: Grandview Lookout Tower is an historic structure offering panoramic views of the Grand Canyon from its elevated vantage point. It provides visitors with a unique perspective of the vast landscape, showcasing the natural beauty of the area from above.

Grandview Point

Location: Located within the Grand Canyon National Park, accessible via the East Rim Drive.
Description: Grandview Point offers an overlook with sweeping views of the Grand Canyon, providing visitors with a breathtaking panorama of the majestic landscape. This point is known for its extensive vistas, allowing for wide-ranging views of the inner canyon and Colorado River.

Hermit's Rest

Location: Located along Hermit Road, at the end of the West Rim Drive in the Grand Canyon National Park.
Description: Hermit's Rest is a circa-1914 faux-rustic rest stop known for its charming architecture and historical significance. Designed by architect Mary Colter, this landmark offers visitors a glimpse into the early 20th-century history of the Grand Canyon, along with stunning views and a peaceful place to rest.

Hopi House

Location: Situated near the Grand Canyon Visitor Center on the South Rim of the Grand Canyon National Park.

Description: Hopi House is a Hopi-style building showcasing native crafts and artwork. This historic structure, also designed by Mary Colter, offers visitors a glimpse into Hopi culture and traditions. The house serves as both a museum and a shop, with beautiful items on display for visitors to admire and purchase.

Hopi Point

Location: Situated along the West Rim Drive of the Grand Canyon National Park.

Description: Hopi Point is renowned for its expansive vistas and is a favored spot for sunrise and sunset views. It offers visitors a perfect location to witness the western sky ablaze with colors during sunset, providing one of the most comprehensive views of the canyon's vast interior.

Indian Garden Ranger Station

Location: Located along the Bright Angel Trail within the Grand Canyon National Park, approximately 4.5 miles down from the South Rim.

Description: The Indian Garden Ranger Station provides advice and assistance to visitors, enhancing the safety and enjoyment of their Grand Canyon experience. It is a vital checkpoint for hikers with a nearby campground for those looking to extend their stay within the canyon.

Maricopa Point

Location: Situated along Hermit Road, west of the Grand Canyon Village on the South Rim.

Description: Maricopa Point offers expansive scenic vistas of the Grand Canyon, allowing visitors to experience the vastness and natural beauty of the area. It provides unique views of the former Orphan Mine and various geological formations.

Mary Colter's Lookout Studio

Location: Perched on the South Rim of the Grand Canyon, near the Bright Angel Lodge.

Description: Mary Colter's Lookout Studio is an architecturally significant structure that blends seamlessly with the canyon's edge. It offers dramatic views of the Grand Canyon and features a gift shop where visitors can purchase souvenirs to commemorate their visit.

Mohave Point

Location: Situated along Hermit Road on the South Rim of the Grand Canyon National Park.

Description: Mohave Point is an exceptional scenic vista that offers panoramic views of the South Rim, with stunning perspectives of the river below. This location provides visitors with a serene spot to enjoy the natural beauty and immense scale of the Grand Canyon.

Navajo Point

Location: Located on the East Rim Drive of the Grand Canyon National Park, close to the Desert View Watchtower.

Description: Navajo Point stands as the highest overlook on the South Rim, providing visitors with sweeping views of the Grand Canyon. From this lofty vantage point, one can marvel at the expansive beauty of the landscape and the intricate layers of geological history.

Pipe Creek Vista

Location: Located along the East Rim Drive, just a short drive from Mather Point in the Grand Canyon National Park.

Description: Pipe Creek Vista offers a scenic viewpoint with panoramic vistas of the Grand Canyon, allowing visitors to immerse themselves in the expansive beauty of the surrounding terrain. It's an accessible spot that provides broad views of the canyon's majesty.

Plateau Point Trail

Location: The trailhead begins at the Bright Angel Trailhead located on the South Rim of the Grand Canyon National Park.

Description: Plateau Point Trail offers a challenging but rewarding hike, presenting breathtaking views of the Grand Canyon from Plateau Point. This scenic hike allows visitors to experience the canyon's beauty up close and personal, providing a unique perspective of its vast expanse.

Powell Point

Location: Situated along the Rim Trail.

Description: Powell Point is celebrated for its exceptional scenic vistas and the historic memorial dedicated to Major John Wesley Powell. It offers visitors a place to admire the panoramic beauty of the Grand Canyon while reflecting on its exploration history.

Shoshone Point Trailhead

Location: Located along Desert View Drive within the Grand Canyon National Park, providing access to Shoshone Point.

Description: Shoshone Point Trailhead marks the start of a relatively less traveled path leading to Shoshone Point, a secluded overlook offering breathtaking views of the Grand Canyon. This area is celebrated for its quiet beauty and panoramic vistas.

Raptor Ranch

Location: Located near the entrance to the Grand Canyon National Park, accessible from the main road leading to the South Rim.

Description: Raptor Ranch is a unique roadside theme park featuring life-sized dinosaur models and exhibits. It offers a fun and educational experience for visitors of all ages, providing insight into the prehistoric world of dinosaurs and the history of raptors.

Skeleton Point

Location: Accessible via the South Kaibab Trail from the South Rim of the Grand Canyon National Park.

Description: Skeleton Point is an elevated lookout offering stunning views of the Colorado River below. The trail to this point is challenging and exposes visitors to the grand scale of the canyon, making it a rewarding destination for experienced hikers.

The Abyss

Location: Located along the Hermit Road route, accessible by shuttle bus or by foot on the Rim Trail within the Grand Canyon National Park.

Description: The Abyss presents an overlook with dramatic views of vertical drop-offs, showcasing the true depth and scale of the Grand Canyon. This spot allows visitors to experience the immense verticality and geological layers of the canyon.

Three Mile Resthouse

Location: Located along the Bright Angel Trail within the Grand Canyon National Park, approximately three miles down from the South Rim.

Description: Three Mile Resthouse offers a rest area for weary hikers descending into or climbing out of the canyon. It provides benches, shade, emergency phone, and seasonal water access, making it an essential stop for hikers needing a break.

Trail of Time

Location: A section of the Rim Trail extending between Yavapai Geology Museum and Grand Canyon Village along the South Rim.

Description: The Trail of Time is an interpretive walking trail that allows visitors to take a leisurely stroll along the canyon's rim while learning about the geological history of the Grand Canyon. The trail features educational exhibits and markers representing different geological periods.

Trail View Overlook

Location: Positioned along the Rim Trail near Grand Canyon Village on the South Rim.
Description: Trail View Overlook offers visitors bird's-eye views of the Grand Canyon, providing a unique vantage point to appreciate the grandeur and vastness of the landscape. This lookout is easily accessible and offers one of the more comprehensive views of the canyon.

Tusayan Museum

Location: Located near the South Rim of the Grand Canyon National Park, close to the Desert View Drive.
Description: The Tusayan Museum offers exhibits that highlight the Native American history and culture of the region, specifically focusing on the ancestral Puebloan people. It provides educational insights into the daily lives and traditions of the people who once inhabited this area.

Tusayan Ruin

Location: Situated a short distance from the Tusayan Museum, near the East Rim of the Grand Canyon National Park.
Description: The Tusayan Ruin provides visitors with a glimpse into the lives of the ancestral Pueblo people through the remains of this ancient village. This site offers a tangible connection to the history and culture of the indigenous inhabitants of the Grand Canyon area.

Verkamp's Visitor Center

Location: Situated at 100 S Entrance Rd, near the Grand Canyon Village on the South Rim.
Description: Verkamp's Visitor Center serves as both a Grand Canyon gift shop and museum. It offers visitors a variety of souvenirs, books, and exhibits that provide insights into the history and geology of the Grand Canyon, making it an educational and memorable stop.

Yaki Point

Location: Located on the South Rim of the Grand Canyon National Park, accessible via the park's shuttle bus service.
Description: Yaki Point is a scenic overlook known for its breathtaking views of the Grand Canyon. The overlook is equipped with restrooms and is accessible by shuttle service, providing a convenient and spectacular viewing spot for visitors.

Yavapai Geology Museum

Location: Situated at Yavapai Point on the South Rim of the Grand Canyon National Park.
Description: The Yavapai Geology Museum offers exhibits that showcase the evolution of rock layers, providing visitors with valuable insights into the geological history of the Grand Canyon. The museum features large windows that offer panoramic views of the canyon.

Yavapai Point

Location: Located near the Yavapai Geology Museum on the South Rim of the Grand Canyon National Park.

Description: Yavapai Point offers unobstructed views of the Grand Canyon, providing visitors with the opportunity to take in the awe-inspiring beauty of this iconic natural wonder. The point offers one of the most comprehensive views of the canyon's interior.

Activities at the Grand Canyon

Hiking

The Grand Canyon offers a variety of hiking trails that cater to different skill levels and preferences. Both the South and North Rims have trails ranging from easy rim-side walks to more strenuous descents into the canyon. The Rim Trail on the South Rim and the Bright Angel Point Trail on the North Rim are perfect for leisurely walks with stunning views. For a more challenging experience, the Bright Angel and North Kaibab trails take you deep into the canyon. It's crucial for hikers to be well-prepared with water, sturdy footwear, and an understanding of the trail's difficulty. Information on trail conditions, safety, and permits for overnight hikes can be found on the National Park Service's website.

Ranger-Led Programs

The National Park Service offers enriching ranger-led programs at the Grand Canyon, suitable for all ages. These programs include guided walks, talks, and evening programs that explore the canyon's geology, ecology, history, and wildlife. These activities are not only educational but also provide deeper insights into the Grand Canyon's significance. Details on program schedules and topics are available at visitor centers and the National Park Service's Grand Canyon website.

Mule Trips

Mule trips are a unique way to experience the Grand Canyon, available at both the South and North Rims. These guided trips range from shorter rides along the rim to multi-day excursions into the canyon, including overnight stays at Phantom Ranch. Advanced reservations are highly recommended as these trips are extremely popular. Pricing, reservation details, and trip descriptions can be found on the official Grand Canyon mule ride concessionaire's website.

Scenic Drives

Scenic drives offer a more relaxed way to enjoy the Grand Canyon's vistas. The South Rim's Desert View Drive and the North Rim's Cape Royal Road provide numerous overlooks with breathtaking views. These drives are accessible by private vehicles, with some restrictions on larger vehicles. Shuttle bus services are also available on specific routes like Hermit Road, offering convenient access to various viewpoints. Vehicle restrictions and shuttle schedules can be found on the National Park Service's website.

River Trips

River trips along the Colorado River through the Grand Canyon are among the most exhilarating ways to experience the canyon's majesty. These journeys provide a unique

perspective of the Grand Canyon, combining adventure with the awe-inspiring beauty of this natural wonder.

White-Water Rafting on the Colorado River

The Colorado River carves its way through the Grand Canyon, offering a variety of white-water rafting experiences that range from mild to wild.

Rafters can experience a range of rapids, from gentle flows to thrilling, challenging whitewater, making these trips a favorite for both novice and experienced rafters alike.

The river journey also allows for an intimate view of the Grand Canyon's geology, as the walls of the canyon tower above and reveal their layers over the course of the trip.

Duration of River Trips

- River trips through the Grand Canyon can vary significantly in length, accommodating different schedules and preferences.

- Shorter trips can last a few days, often covering a section of the river and offering a brief but exhilarating experience of the canyon.
- Longer expeditions can last up to three weeks, allowing for a comprehensive journey through much of the Grand Canyon. These extended trips offer a deeper connection with the river and the canyon, including opportunities for side hikes, camping under the stars, and a full immersion into the wilderness. For more information about companies that provides river concessioners trips through Grand Canyon, Lees Ferry to Diamond Creek (226 river miles/364 km) visit
https://www.nps.gov/grca/planyourvisit/river-concessioners.htm

Permits and Arranging a Trip

- Due to the popularity and environmental sensitivity of river trips in the Grand Canyon, permits are required. These permits are highly sought after and are typically obtained through a lottery system managed by the National Park Service.
  Alternatively, visitors can book a trip through commercial tour operators. These outfitters offer a range of packages and take care of all the logistics, from equipment to guiding services, making the trip accessible to those who may not have prior rafting experience.

There are several commercial operators are authorized by the National Park Service to provide guided rafting tours. These tours range from single-day trips to multi-week adventures, offering a unique way to experience the Colorado River and the Grand Canyon. Here are some recommended operators:

1. **O.A.R.S. Grand Canyon, Inc.:** Known for their variety of rafting options, including both motorized and non-motorized rafts.
   Website: https://www.oars.com/grand-canyon/
2. **Arizona River Runners:** Offers both full-canyon and partial-canyon trips with a choice of motorized rafts, oar-powered rafts, or paddle rafts.
3. Website: https://www.raftarizona.com/
4. **Grand Canyon Whitewater:** Provides all-inclusive rafting trips with options for hiking and camping along the river.
   Website: https://www.grandcanyonwhitewater.com/
5. **Canyoneers, Inc.:** The oldest Grand Canyon river running company under continuous family ownership, offering a range of trip options.
6. Website: https://www.canyoneers.com/
7. **Western River Expeditions:** Offers a variety of rafting experiences, including both motorized and oar-powered trips. Website: https://www.westernriver.com/

Skywalk and West Rim

The Grand Canyon Skywalk is an engineering marvel. This horseshoe-shaped glass bridge extends 70 feet out over the rim of the canyon, providing visitors with a thrilling experience. Standing on the Skywalk, one can look down through the transparent floor to the canyon floor 4,000 feet below, offering a unique and breathtaking perspective.

The Skywalk is more than just a viewing platform; it's an example of contemporary design seamlessly blending with the natural world. The structure is designed to be both minimally invasive and to offer maximum views, ensuring a truly unforgettable experience.

Other Attractions at the West Rim

Beyond the Skywalk, the West Rim offers a variety of attractions and activities that provide different ways to experience the canyon.

Helicopter Tours: These tours offer an aerial view of the Grand Canyon, providing a sweeping perspective of the vast landscape. Flying over the canyon, visitors can appreciate its magnitude and the varied topography of the area.

Zip-lining: For the adventure-seekers, zip-lining at the West Rim offers an exhilarating way to experience the Grand Canyon. It combines the thrill of speed and height with spectacular views.

Scenic Viewpoints: The West Rim has several viewpoints that offer stunning vistas of the canyon. These viewpoints are less crowded than those at the South and North Rims, providing a more relaxed experience.

Wildlife and Geological History

Wildlife in the Grand Canyon

The park is a sanctuary for a diverse array of wildlife, adapted to its unique environments from the river corridors to the canyon rims.

Bighorn Sheep: These agile animals are often seen on the rocky outcrops of the canyon, adept at navigating the steep terrain.

Mule Deer: Commonly spotted in the forested rim areas and occasionally in the inner canyon, mule deer are a graceful and familiar sight.

Bird Species: The Grand Canyon is a haven for birdwatchers, with over 450 species of birds recorded. It's home to the California condor, one of North America's most endangered birds, along with other species like the peregrine falcon, the canyon wren, and the red-tailed hawk.

Other Wildlife: The park also supports populations of coyotes, elk, mountain lions, and a variety of smaller mammals and reptiles.

Geological History

The Grand Canyon is a geological library, with each layer of rock telling a story of Earth's past. The exposed strata provide a visible record of nearly two billion years of geological history, showcasing dramatic shifts in the environment over time.

The Vishnu Basement Rocks at the bottom of the canyon are some of the oldest, dating back around 1.8 billion years. They give us a glimpse into the early history of the Earth's crust. As you move up through the layers, you encounter formations from different geological periods, each adding to the narrative of the Earth's development. The more recent Kaibab Limestone on the rim is around 270 million years old, depicting a much younger chapter in the story.

Lodging Options
Recommended Lodges and Hotels

Historic Lodges: The Grand Canyon is home to several historic lodges, especially at the South Rim, like the famous El Tovar Hotel, which offers luxury accommodations with stunning canyon views. Bright Angel Lodge and Phantom Ranch (at the bottom of the canyon) are other notable options, each with its unique charm and history.

Modern Hotels: In addition to historic lodges, there are modern hotels and lodges available, providing contemporary amenities and comfort. These are located both within the park and in nearby towns like Tusayan, near the South Rim, and Jacob Lake, near the North Rim.

Estimate Cost: Prices can vary widely based on the type of accommodation and the season. For example:

- The El Tovar Hotel, known for its luxury offerings, can range from approximately $200 to over $500 per night.
- Bright Angel Lodge and Phantom Ranch are generally more affordable, with prices starting around $100 per night, but can vary based on room type and season.
- For current rates and reservations, visit the official Grand Canyon Lodging website: https://www.grandcanyonlodges.com/

Hotels Near the Park: Accommodations in nearby towns like Tusayan or Jacob Lake offer various options, from budget motels to higher-end hotels, with prices typically ranging from $100 to $300 per night.

Camping

Campgrounds: There are several campgrounds within the Grand Canyon National Park. The South Rim's Mather Campground and the North Rim's North Rim Campground are popular choices, offering facilities like restrooms and water access.

Backcountry Camping: For those seeking a more rugged and remote experience, backcountry camping is available. This requires a permit from the National Park Service and is ideal for adventurous travelers looking to explore deeper into the canyon.

Reservations and Planning

Reservations for both lodges and campgrounds are highly recommended, especially during the peak tourist seasons (spring through fall). Accommodations within the park can fill up quickly, sometimes requiring booking several months in advance.

Reservations can usually be made online or via phone. The National Park Service website provides detailed information on lodging and camping options, including how to make reservations.

For those unable to secure accommodations within the park, there are several lodging options in nearby towns, which can also serve as convenient bases for exploring the Grand Canyon.

Estimate Cost

Campgrounds: Fees for campgrounds like Mather Campground on the South Rim and the North Rim Campground are typically around $18 to $25 per night. These are standard rates for a campsite and may vary slightly.

Backcountry Camping: Requires a permit from the National Park Service. The permit fee is $10 per permit plus $8 per person per night camped below the rim and $8 per group per night camped above the rim.

Contact and Website: For detailed information, visit the National Park Service's official Grand Canyon website https://www.nps.gov/grca/index.htm. The website provides comprehensive information on activities, planning your visit, lodging, and up-to-date park news. For specific inquiries, contact information for park offices and visitor centers is also available on the website.

General Park Information: (928) 638-7888

Public Affairs Office: (928) 638-7779

Backcountry Information Center: (928) 638-7875 between 8 am and 5 pm Monday through Friday, except on federal holidays

River Permits Office: (800) 959-9164 or (928) 638-7884

Comprehensive List of Accommodations within the Park
For information on pricing and availability for various accommodations, please scan the QR Code.

Bright Angel Lodge

Description: Bright Angel Lodge is a landmark property that features a range of accommodations from cozy rooms to rustic cabins, catering to different preferences and budgets. This 1-star hotel combines comfort with history, providing guests with a unique stay at one of the world's most iconic natural wonders.

Amenities: Free parking, free Wi-Fi, air-conditioned rooms, on-site dining options, and close proximity to the Grand Canyon.

Starting Rate: Rooms starting from USD 180 per night.

Best Western Premier Grand Canyon Squire Inn

Description: The Best Western Premier Grand Canyon Squire Inn is a modern 4-star hotel featuring a range of amenities for a comfortable and enjoyable stay. With a pool, on-site dining, and other luxurious amenities, guests can relax and unwind after a day of exploration.

Amenities: Pool, free parking, free Wi-Fi, air-conditioned rooms, on-site dining, fitness center.

Starting Rate: Rooms starting from USD 130 per night.

El Tovar Hotel

Description: El Tovar Hotel is a historic 3-star hotel that has been providing luxury accommodations since its opening. With its unique blend of charm, history, and elegance, guests can enjoy a high-end stay with modern comforts while being steps away from the Grand Canyon.

Amenities: Free parking, free Wi-Fi, air-conditioned rooms, fine dining options, and exceptional service.

Starting Rate: Rooms starting from USD 450 per night.

Grand Canyon Plaza Hotel

Description: The Grand Canyon Plaza Hotel is a casual 3-star hotel that provides a comfortable and relaxing environment for guests. With amenities like a pool and spa, it's a great place to unwind after a day of adventure. The free canyon shuttle service makes it easy to explore the area's natural beauty.

Amenities: Pool, spa, free parking, free Wi-Fi, free canyon shuttle service.

Starting Rate: Rooms starting from USD 180 per night.

Holiday Inn Express & Suites Grand Canyon, an IHG Hotel

Description: Holiday Inn Express & Suites Grand Canyon is a modest 3-star hotel offering a budget-friendly option without sacrificing comfort. Guests can enjoy a free breakfast each morning before heading out to explore the Grand Canyon, along with other amenities to make their stay enjoyable.

Amenities: Pool, free parking, free breakfast, free Wi-Fi.

Starting Rate: Rooms starting from USD 200 per night.

Kachina Lodge

Description: Kachina Lodge is a 2-star hotel providing unpretentious and comfortable lodging. It's a straightforward choice for those wishing to stay within the park without the frills of luxury accommodations but with all the necessary amenities.

Amenities: Free parking, free Wi-Fi, air-conditioned rooms.

Starting Rate: Rooms starting from USD 400 per night.

Maswik Lodge

Description: Maswik Lodge is a 2-star hotel providing low-key and relaxed rooms in a complex set amidst a pine forest. It offers a comfortable stay with basic amenities, making it an ideal choice for families and travelers looking for a peaceful environment.

Amenities: Free parking, free Wi-Fi, air-conditioned rooms.

Starting Rate: Rooms starting from USD 400 per night.

Phantom Ranch

Description: Phantom Ranch is a historic lodge offering basic rooms and dormitory-style accommodations. This 2-star hotel provides a unique opportunity to stay overnight within the depths of the Grand Canyon, surrounded by breathtaking natural beauty.

Amenities: Basic lodging, restaurant (reservations required), access to water and restrooms. Note: There is no direct vehicle access; guests must hike or ride a mule to reach the location.

Red Feather Lodge

Description: Red Feather Lodge is a modern 2-star hotel that combines comfort and convenience for a memorable stay. It features a seasonal pool where guests can relax after a day of exploring, along with other essential amenities to enhance your visit..

Amenities: Seasonal pool, free parking, free Wi-Fi, air-conditioned rooms.

Starting Rate: Rooms starting from USD 150 per night.

Thunderbird Lodge

Description: Thunderbird Lodge is a 1-star, no-frills hotel providing essential amenities for a comfortable stay. Ideal for visitors looking for straightforward accommodation, the lodge offers free Wi-Fi among other basic comforts, allowing guests to stay connected while immersed in the natural beauty of the canyon.

Starting Rate: Rooms starting from USD 300 per night.

The Grand Hotel at the Grand Canyon

Description: The Grand Hotel at the Grand Canyon is a rustic yet modern 3-star hotel offering comfortable lodging with a pool and on-site dining options. The hotel combines a cozy, cabin-like ambiance with modern amenities, making it an ideal retreat after a day of exploring the Grand Canyon.

Amenities: Pool, free parking, free Wi-Fi, air-conditioned rooms, on-site dining.

Starting Rate: Rooms starting from USD 250 per night.

Yavapai Lodge

Description: Yavapai Lodge offers basic lodging with a low-key atmosphere, perfect for travelers seeking simplicity and convenience. This 2-star hotel features comfortable rooms and an on-site restaurant, providing essential amenities for a pleasant stay.

Amenities: Free parking, free Wi-Fi, air-conditioned rooms, on-site restaurant serving breakfast and other meals.

Starting Rate: Rooms starting from USD 170 per night.

Bright Angel Campground

Location: Located at the bottom of the Grand Canyon, adjacent to the Colorado River, accessible via the South Kaibab Trail or the Bright Angel Trail.

Description: Bright Angel Campground offers creekside campsites set in the stunning canyon wilderness. It's an ideal spot for hikers looking to experience the beauty of the Grand Canyon from within. The campground provides basic amenities in a remote setting, offering a unique overnight outdoor experience.

Amenities: Potable water, toilets, emergency phone, and ranger station.

Cottonwood Campground

Location: Situated within a national park, typically along the North Kaibab Trail in the Grand Canyon National Park.

Description: Cottonwood Campground is a simple, back-to-basics campground located in a serene setting within the national park. It's ideal for hikers trekking between the North Rim and the Colorado River, providing necessary rest and amenities.

Amenities: Potable water, toilets, and picnic tables.

Havasupai Gardens Campground

Location: Situated along the Bright Angel Trail within the Grand Canyon National Park.

Description: Havasupai Gardens Campground, also known as Indian Garden, provides forested campsites offering shade and respite for hikers trekking the Bright Angel Trail. This campground serves as a mid-point rest area and offers basic facilities amidst stunning natural surroundings.

Amenities: Water, picnic tables, toilets, and ranger station for assistance and emergencies.

North Rim Campground

Location: Located within the Grand Canyon National Park, offering serene settings and easier access from the North Rim.

Description: North Rim Campground provides park visitors with tent and RV sites surrounded by the quiet beauty of the Grand Canyon's North Rim. This campground is perfect for those seeking a more secluded and less crowded camping experience.

Amenities: Free parking, tent and RV sites, toilets, and availability of Wi-Fi in certain areas.

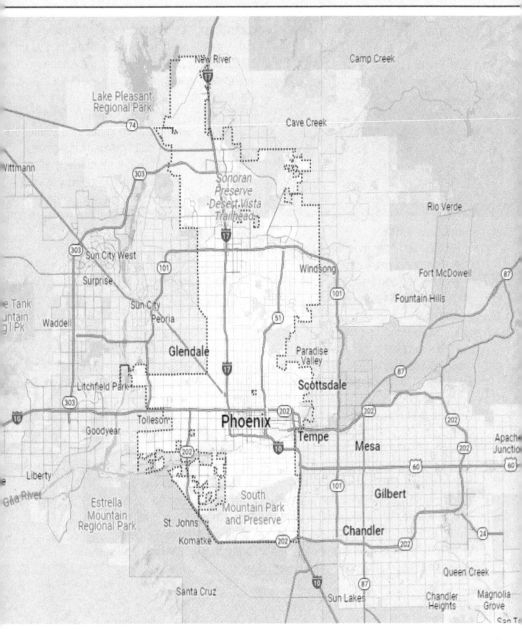

Phoenix, the capital and largest city of Arizona, offers a unique blend of urban sophistication and outdoor adventure, set against a backdrop of a vast desert landscape. Known for its vibrant arts scene, culinary diversity, and sprawling layout, Phoenix is a dynamic city that invites exploration.
The list below includes a wide range of tourist attractions located in Phoenix and the surrounding vicinity.

Museums and Cultural Institutions
Adobe Mountain Train Museum

Location: 23280 N. 43rd Ave., Glendale, Arizona. Situated just outside Phoenix, this unique museum forms part of the Adobe Mountain Desert Park, alongside other railroad heritage organizations.

Description: The Adobe Mountain Train Museum offers visitors an in-depth look into the historical significance of railroads in Arizona. Located in a repurposed park ranger station, the museum is a treasure trove of railway artifacts and exhibits. It stands as a testament to the evolution and impact of train travel in the region.

Exhibits Include:
- Detailed train models showcasing different scales.
- Historical railroad artifacts, including a conductor's cap, railroad spikes, and lanterns.
- The bell and headlight from a Porter 0-4-0 18" gauge locomotive, highlighting the technological advancements in railway engines.

Activities:
- Explore the rich history of railroads through various exhibits.
- Enjoy guided tours available by appointment to gain deeper insights.
- Participate in special events and educational programs during the open season.

Best For: Train enthusiasts, history buffs, families, and students interested in the cultural and technological history of Arizona's railroads.

Season and Hours: Open primarily during the winter months, from mid-September to early May. Regular hours are Sundays from 11:00 AM to 3:00 PM. Additional visits can be scheduled by appointment.

Admission: Entry to the museum is free, but donations are gratefully accepted to support its operations and preservation efforts.

Additional Information: The museum is part of the larger Adobe Mountain Desert Park, which includes the Sahuaro Central Railroad Heritage Preservation Society, the Arizona Model Railroading Society, and the Maricopa Live Steamers. Visitors can enjoy a comprehensive railway experience by exploring these associated societies.

Website: https://adobemtndesertrrpark.com/

Arizona Capitol Museum

Location: 1700 W Washington St, Phoenix, AZ

Description: The Arizona Capitol Museum is a vibrant center dedicated to showcasing the rich and diverse history of Arizona and its governmental evolution. As a landmark listed on the National Register of Historic Places, the building itself is a piece of history, offering a compelling backdrop to the various exhibits and stories within.

Exhibits Include:
- An exploration of the Arizona State Capitol's history.
- Insight into the development and function of Arizona's government.
- Detailed accounts of the lives of Arizona's governors and key historical figures.

Opening Hours: Opens at 9 AM – 4 PM on Monday to Friday. 10AM to 2PM on Saturday and closed on Sunday.

https://azcapitolmuseum.gov/

Arizona Commemorative Air Force Museum

Location: 2017 N Greenfield Rd, Mesa, AZ
Description: As the 10th unit of the Commemorative Air Force and one of its largest units worldwide, this museum is a treasure trove of aviation history, showcasing aircraft from World War I through the Vietnam era.
Exhibits Include:
- The B-17G "Sentimental Journey," one of the most meticulously restored B-17 Flying Fortresses still flying today.
- The iconic B-25 Mitchell bomber.
- The legendary P-51 Mustang fighter.
- The workhorse C-47 Skytrain cargo plane.
- The classic PT-17 Stearman biplane.

Opening Hours: Wednesday to Sunday 10AM – 4PM. Closed on Monday & Tuesday.
Website: https://www.azcaf.org/

Arizona Heritage Center

Location: 1300 N College Ave, Tempe, AZ 85281
Description: Engage with Arizona's rich history and cultural heritage through interactive exhibits at the Arizona Heritage Center. This museum offers a deep dive into the state's past, showcasing everything from early indigenous cultures to modern advancements.
Activities: Visitors can explore Arizona's past through interactive displays, historical artifacts, and engaging stories.
Opening Hours: Tuesday: 10 AM - 5 PM
Website: www.arizonahistoricalsociety.org/museum/arizona-heritage-center/

Arizona Museum of Natural History

Location: 53 N Macdonald, Mesa, AZ 85213
Description: Dive into the natural history of the Southwest at the Arizona Museum of Natural History. Discover the prehistoric world of dinosaurs, the rich biodiversity of the region, and the geological formations that define the Southwest.
Activities: Learn about the ancient dinosaurs, native plants and animals, and explore the geological wonders of the Southwest through various exhibits.
Opening Hours: Daily: 10 AM - 5 PM
Website: www.arizonamuseumofnaturalhistory.org

Arizona Science Center

Location: 600 E Washington St, Phoenix, AZ 85004
Description: The Arizona Science Center offers an educational adventure for all ages with hands-on science exhibits. Engage with scientific principles through interactive displays and experiments across various disciplines.
Activities: Participate in exciting experiments, explore interactive exhibits, and discover the wonders of science in areas such as physics, biology, and astronomy.
Opening Hours: Daily: 9:30 AM - 4 PM | **Website:** www.azscience.org

Arizona State University Art Museum

Location: 51 E 10th St, Tempe, AZ 85281
Description: The ASU Art Museum showcases a wide range of contemporary art exhibits, offering a space for visitors to engage with current artistic expressions and innovative creations from diverse artists.
Activities: Immerse yourself in contemporary art, interact with thought-provoking exhibits, and connect with the creative visions of modern artists.
Opening Hours: Wednesday - Sunday: 11 AM - 5 PM
Website: www.asuartmuseum.org

Children's Museum of Phoenix

Location: 215 N 7th St, Phoenix, AZ 85003
Description: This museum is dedicated to child-focused learning, featuring interactive exhibits that encourage play, creativity, and curiosity.
Activities: Children can engage in hands-on activities, participate in workshops, and attend special events designed to spark their imagination and learning.
Opening Hours: Tuesday - Sunday: 9 AM - 4 PM
Website: www.childrensmuseumofphoenix.org

Deer Valley Petroglyph Preserve

Location: 3711 W Deer Valley Rd, Phoenix, AZ 85086
Description: This preserve is home to a vast collection of prehistoric petroglyphs, offering a unique glimpse into the lives of the Hohokam people and the region's ancient past.
Activities: Visitors can hike scenic trails, view ancient rock carvings, and participate in educational programs about the area's prehistoric cultures.
Opening Hours: Tues - Saturday: 8 AM – 2 PM
Website: www.deervalley.asu.edu

Cave Creek Museum

Location: 6140 E Skyline Dr, Cave Creek, AZ 85331
Description: The Cave Creek Museum delves into the history and culture of Cave Creek and the surrounding area, offering insights into the lives of its indigenous inhabitants, early settlers, and characters from the Wild West era.
Activities: Visitors can learn through exhibits, educational programs, and explore the local history and heritage.
Opening Hours: Wednesday - Saturday: 10 AM - 4 PM
Website: www.cavecreekmuseum.org

Chandler Museum

Location: 300 S Chandler Village Dr, Chandler, AZ 85224
Description: The Chandler Museum showcases the rich history of Chandler, highlighting its evolution from agricultural roots to a modern technology hub.
Activities: Explore the city's history through engaging exhibits and learn about Chandler's development and cultural heritage.
Opening Hours: Tuesday - Saturday: 9 AM - 4:30 PM
Website: www.chandleraz.gov/explore/arts-and-culture/chandler-museum

Heard Museum

Location: 2301 N Central Ave, Phoenix, AZ 85004
Description: The Heard Museum is dedicated to the art and culture of American Indian tribes, with a focus on the Southwest. It serves as a platform for Native art and voices.
Activities: Visitors can explore exhibits of art, textiles, pottery, and jewelry and participate in cultural events, workshops, and lectures.
Opening Hours: Monday - Saturday: 9 AM - 5 PM, Sunday: Noon - 5 PM
Website: www.heard.org

Heritage & Science Park/Historic Heritage Square

Location: 1150 W Baseline Rd, Tempe, AZ 85283
Description: A multifaceted venue combining history, science, and children's activities, where visitors can immerse themselves in Arizona's rich past and scientific discoveries.
Activities: Explore historic buildings, ride a carousel, visit a model railroad display, and engage with interactive exhibits about Arizona's history and science.
Opening Hours: Tuesday - Saturday: 9 AM - 5 PM, Sunday: Noon - 5 PM

49

Huhugam Heritage Center

Location: 1200 W Gila River Dr, Chandler, AZ 85248
Description: The center preserves and showcases the history and culture of the Gila River Indian Community, focusing on the Huhugam people (Pima and Maricopa).
Activities: Learn about the community through exhibits, demonstrations, and events.
Opening Hours: Tuesday - Friday: 10 AM - 4 PM
Website: www.gilariver.org/index.php/enterprises/huhugam-heritage-center

i.d.e.a. Museum

Location: 150 W Pepper Pl, Mesa, AZ 85201
Description: The i.d.e.a. Museum is dedicated to fostering creativity and curiosity among children of all ages through interactive art exhibits and activities.
Activities: Children can engage in creative play, partake in art-inspired activities, and learn about various artistic concepts in an enriching environment.
Opening Hours: Thursdays - Saturdays: Timed entry at 10 AM, 12 PM, and 2 PM; Sundays: 12 PM & 2 PM; Closed Mondays-Wednesdays
Website: www.ideamuseum.org

Mesa Contemporary Arts Museum

Location: 1 E Main St, Mesa, AZ 85201
Description: This museum showcases a wide array of contemporary art from both established and emerging artists, providing a platform for diverse artistic expressions.
Activities: Visitors can immerse themselves in contemporary art exhibitions, participate in artist discussions and workshops, and experience the forefront of artistic innovation.
Opening Hours: Tuesday - Saturday: 10 AM - 5 PM, Sunday: Noon - 5 PM
Website: www.mesaartscenter.com

Mesa Historical Museum

Location: 2345 N Horne, Mesa, AZ 85207
Description: The Mesa Historical Museum is committed to preserving and interpreting the rich history of Mesa, Arizona, from its agricultural beginnings to its present-day status.
Activities: Explore the history of Mesa through exhibits that cover the city's agricultural roots, early settlers, and urban development.
Opening Hours: Tuesday - Saturday: 9 AM - 4:30 PM

Musical Instrument Museum

Location: 4725 E Mayo Blvd, Phoenix, AZ 85054
Description: This museum houses a globally diverse collection of musical instruments, offering a unique exploration of the universal language of music.
Activities: Explore global musical instruments, enjoy live performances, and participate in interactive activities and exhibits.
Opening Hours: Daily: 9 AM - 5 PM
Website: www.mim.org

Phoenix Art Museum

Location: 1625 N Central Ave, Phoenix, AZ 85004
Description: The Phoenix Art Museum stands as a world-renowned institution, boasting a vast collection of over 20,000 works of art from various centuries and cultures.
Activities: Visitors can explore diverse exhibits ranging from medieval European to contemporary American art, participate in guided tours, and attend a variety of special events.
Opening Hours: Tuesday - Sunday: 10 AM - 5 PM, Closed Mondays
Website: www.phxart.org/visit/

Phoenix Police Museum

Location: 221 E Jackson St, Phoenix, AZ 85004
Description: The museum is dedicated to preserving the rich history of the Phoenix Police Department and law enforcement in Arizona.
Activities: Discover the history of policing through exhibits featuring police equipment, uniforms, and historical artifacts.
Opening Hours: Tuesday - Saturday: 10 AM - 4 PM
Website: www.phoenixpolicemuseum.org

S'edav Va'aki Museum (formerly Pueblo Grande Museum)

Location: 4619 E Washington St, Phoenix, AZ 85034
Description: This museum showcases the history and culture of the Hohokam people, an ancient community that inhabited the area over 1,500 years ago.
Opening Hours:
October through April: Monday - Saturday: 9 AM - 4:45 PM, Sunday: 1 PM - 4:45 PM;
May through September: Closed Sundays and Mondays
Website: www.phoenix.gov/parks/arts-culture-history/sedav-vaaki

Scottsdale Historical Museum

Location: 3833 N Marshall Way, Scottsdale, AZ 85251
Description: The museum focuses on the history and development of Scottsdale, from its beginnings as an agricultural community to its current status as a renowned resort destination.
Opening Hours: Wednesday - Saturday: 10 AM - 5 PM. Sunday: Noon – 4 PM
Website: www.scottsdalehistory.org

Rosson House Museum at Heritage Square

Location: 113 N 6th St, Phoenix, AZ 85004
Description: The Rosson House Museum is a beautifully restored 1895 Queen Anne Victorian house that offers a glimpse into the lives of Phoenix's early families and their history.
Activities: Visitors can take guided tours of the fully restored house to learn about the lifestyle, culture, and architecture of early Phoenix residents.
Opening Hours: Wednesday - Saturday: 10 AM - 5 PM, Sunday: 12 PM - 5 PM
Website: www.heritagesquarephx.org

Tovrea Castle at Carraro Heights

Location: 2002 E Van Buren St, Phoenix, AZ 85006
Description: Tovrea Castle is a distinctive non-profit museum located in a historic castle-like structure, offering visitors a unique glimpse into the eclectic history and architecture of early 20th-century Phoenix.
Activities: Explore the castle's intriguing history, architectural details, and enjoy the panoramic views from the rooftop.
Opening Hours: Wednesday - Saturday: 10 AM - 4 PM, Sunday: Noon - 4 PM
Website: www.tovreacastletours.com/castle-tours/

Entertainment and Experiences

Arizona Balloon Safaris

Address: 29834 N Cave Creek Rd, Cave Creek, AZ 85331
Description: Embark on an unforgettable adventure with Arizona Balloon Safaris. Ascend into the sky aboard a hot air balloon and witness breathtaking panoramic views of the iconic Sonoran Desert. Experience the tranquility of floating amidst the desert landscape and create lasting memories.
Website: www.arizonaballoonsafaris.com

Arizona Boardwalk

Address: 9500 E Vía de Ventura, Scottsdale, AZ 85256
Description: Immerse yourself in the vibrant entertainment hub of Arizona Boardwalk. Discover a diverse array of marine life at the captivating aquarium, indulge in delicious food options at various restaurants, or browse through unique shops. Challenge yourself with exciting arcade games, putt your way through a fun mini-golf course, and create memorable moments with family and friends.
Website: www.azboardwalk.com

Arizona Falls

Address: 5802 E Indian School Rd, Phoenix, AZ 85018

Description: Step back in time and explore the captivating Arizona Falls. This historic landmark boasts cascading waterfalls flowing down a man-made rock formation, offering a scenic escape within the city. Follow the walking paths, delve into the site's rich history, and be captivated by the picturesque surroundings.

Website: www.phoenix.gov

Arizona Food Tours

Address: 7333 E Scottsdale Mall, Scottsdale, AZ 85251

Description: Embark on a delectable culinary adventure with Arizona Food Tours. Explore Scottsdale's vibrant food scene alongside knowledgeable guides and tantalize your taste buds with samplings from various restaurants and local eateries. Immerse yourself in the city's unique culinary culture and savor the diverse flavors offered by Scottsdale's hidden gems.

Website: www.arizonafoodtours.com

Bronze Horse Fountain by Bob Parks

Address: 5th Avenue & Scottsdale Rd, Scottsdale, AZ 85251

Description: A stunning public art display, the Bronze Horse Fountain features five rearing Arabian horses, masterfully sculpted by artist Bob Parks. This iconic fountain is a tribute to the beauty and spirit of the Arabian horse.

Activities:

- Admire the detailed artistic interpretation of Arabian horses.
- Capture scenic photos with the fountain as a beautiful backdrop.
- Explore the surrounding shops and restaurants on 5th Avenue.

Opening Hours: Open 24 hours

Butterfly Wonderland

Address: 9500 East Vía de Ventura F100, Scottsdale.

Description: This butterfly atrium in Scottsdale, Arizona, is home to thousands of butterflies from all over the world. It's a great place to learn about these fascinating creatures.

Opening Hours: Daily 9AM - 5PM |

Website: butterflywonderland.com/

Carnival of Illusion

Address: 2400 E Missouri Ave, Phoenix, AZ 85016

Description: Step into a world of magic at the Carnival of Illusion, an intimate and enchanting venue featuring world-class illusionists and mind-bending performances that will leave you in awe.

Opening Hours: Showtimes vary, visit website for details.

Website: www.carnivalofillusion.com

CREATE at Arizona Science Center

Address: 600 E Washington St, Phoenix, AZ 85004
(located within the Arizona Science Center)
Description: CREATE at Arizona Science Center is a dynamic space designed to foster creativity and innovation, offering hands-on activities and interactive exhibits that merge science, art, and technology.
Opening Hours: Daily: 9:30 AM - 4 PM
https://www.azscience.org/attractions/create-makerspace/

Crayola Experience Chandler

Address: 3111 W Chandler Blvd Suite 2154, Chandler, AZ 85224
Description: Ignite your child's creativity and imagination at the Crayola Experience Chandler. This vibrant, interactive play space is filled with various colorful activities, allowing kids to explore their artistic talents and express themselves through a spectrum of colors.
Opening Hours:
Monday - Thursday: 10 AM - 4 PM | Friday - Saturday: 10 AM - 5 PM
Sunday: 11 AM - 4 PM | **Website:** www.crayolaexperience.com

Goldfield Ghost Town and Mine Tours Inc.

Address: 4650 N Mammoth Mine Rd, Apache Junction, AZ 85220
Description: Step back in time at Goldfield Ghost Town, an authentically preserved Wild West town offering a glimpse into the lives of miners, cowboys, and outlaws of yesteryears.
Activities:
- Take a guided mine tour to learn about the history of gold mining in the area.
- Try your luck panning for gold and discover hidden treasures.
- Experience the Wild West firsthand with a live-action shootout reenactment.

Opening Hours: Daily: 10 AM - 5 PM | **Website:** www.visitchandler.com

iFLY Indoor Skydiving - Phoenix

Address: 9206 Talking Stick Way, Scottsdale, AZ 85250
Description: Experience the unparalleled thrill of skydiving without having to jump from an airplane at iFLY Indoor Skydiving Phoenix. This state-of-the-art facility offers a safe and exhilarating way to experience human flight, suitable for all ages.
Opening Hours:
- Monday - Thursday: 1 PM - 9 PM,
- Friday: 1 PM - 10 PM,
- Saturday: 10 AM - 10 PM,
- Sunday: 11 AM - 8 PM

Web: www.indoorskydivingsource.com

Inferno Escape Room

Address: 2155 E University Dr #210, Tempe, AZ 85281
Description: Test your teamwork and problem-solving skills at Inferno Escape Room. Engage in an immersive experience with various themed rooms, each offering unique challenges and puzzles to conquer within a set time limit.
Opening Hours: Varies by location and day; please check the website for specific times.
Website: www.infernoescaperoom.com

Laser + Mirror Maze

Address: 9500 East Vía de Ventura #200, Scottsdale, AZ 85256
Description: Dive into a world of adventure with Laser + Mirror Maze locations across Arizona. Experience the thrill of navigating through challenging laser tag arenas and mind-bending mirror mazes designed for family fun and adventure.
Opening Hours: Sunday-Thursday 10AM - 5PM, Friday-Saturday 10AM - 6PM
Website: http://www.odyseamirrormaze.com/

LEGOLAND Discovery Center Arizona

Address: 5000 S Arizona Mills Cir STE 135, Tempe, AZ 85282
Description: Ignite your imagination at LEGOLAND Discovery Center Arizona, a playful and interactive space designed for LEGO enthusiasts of all ages. Explore, build, and be amazed in a world filled with LEGO adventures.
Opening Hours: Daily: 10 AM - 5 PM
www.legolanddiscoverycenter.com/arizona

OdySea Aquarium

Location: 9500 East Vía de Ventura Suite A-100, Scottsdale, AZ 85256.
Description: OdySea Aquarium is a premier destination in Scottsdale, showcasing the wonders of the aquatic world through stunning exhibits, interactive experiences, and a captivating 3D movie.
Highlights:
Dramatic Exhibits: Explore various themed areas, including the Open Ocean, SeaTREK® Underwater Exploration Experience (additional fee applies), and the Playa del Carmen Exhibit. Witness the awe-inspiring underwater world and the incredible creatures that inhabit it.
Accessibility: Wheelchair-accessible parking,

entrance, seating, and restrooms are available for your convenience.
Opening Hours: Daily: 09 AM - 7 PM | **Website:** https://www.odyseaaquarium.com/

Address: 1302 W Washington St, Phoenix, AZ 85003
Description: Encounter a diverse range of animals from around the world at the Phoenix Zoo. This vibrant environment allows visitors to explore various habitats, witness fascinating creatures, and participate in interactive experiences designed for all ages..
Opening Hours: Daily: 9:00 AM - 5:00 PM
Website: www.phoenixzoo.org

Ripley's Believe It or Not! ®

Address: 9500 East Vía de Ventura Suite D-220, Scottsdale, AZ 85256
Description: Prepare to be amazed and bewildered at Ripley's Believe It or Not!® in Scottsdale. Venture through exhibits that showcase a collection of unusual artifacts, mind-boggling oddities, and incredible stories from around the globe.
Opening Hours: Daily: 10:00 AM - 5:00 PM
Website: www.ripleysaz.com

Pangaea Land of the Dinosaurs

Address: 9500 East Vía de Ventura c100, Scottsdale, AZ 85256
Description: Step into the prehistoric world of Pangaea Land of the Dinosaurs and embark on an educational and thrilling journey back in time. Encounter life-sized animatronic dinosaurs, learn about their lives, and explore exhibits showcasing these magnificent creatures.
Opening Hours: Daily: 10 AM - 6 PM
Website: https://pangaealandofthedinosaurs.com/

Superstition Zipline

Address: 4650 N Mammoth Mine Rd, Apache Junction, AZ 85220
Description: Experience the exhilarating thrill of soaring through the air on a zipline adventure at Superstition Zipline. Embark on a journey with guided tours, conquer exciting ziplines, and enjoy breathtaking panoramic views of the Superstition Mountains.
Opening Hours: Varies by season and day; please check the website for specific times.
Website: www.superstitionzipline.com

Parks and Nature

Anthem Community Park

Address: 41703 N Gavilan Peak Pkwy, Anthem.
This park in Anthem, Arizona, features a pond, playground, and trails. It's a great place for families to enjoy the outdoors.

Arizona Falls

Address: 5802 E Indian School Rd, Phoenix.
This historic site in Phoenix, Arizona, features cascading waterfalls flowing down a man-made rock formation. It offers a scenic escape within the city.

Base & Meridian Wildlife Area

Address: S Avondale Blvd, Avondale.
This wildlife area in Avondale, Arizona, is a great place to go bird watching and hiking. It protects over 3,000 acres of Sonoran Desert habitat.

Cactus Park

Address: 7202 E Cactus Rd, Scottsdale.
This park in Scottsdale, Arizona, features a pool, gym, and courts. It's a great place to go for a swim, workout, or play some sports.

Camelback Mountain

Address: Echo Canyon Recreation Area, 4925 E McDonald Dr, Phoenix, AZ
A prominent landmark and popular hiking destination, Camelback Mountain offers challenging trails and panoramic views of the Phoenix area. A must-visit for outdoor enthusiasts, but trails can be strenuous, so adequate preparation is essential.

Carefree Desert Gardens

Address: 101 Easy St, Carefree, AZ
Explore the Carefree Desert Gardens, featuring an array of desert plants and a unique sundial. It's an ideal spot for those looking to immerse themselves in the serene beauty of the desert. Open 24 hours.

Chaparral Park

Address: 5401 Hayden Rd, Scottsdale, AZ
Chaparral Park in Scottsdale, Arizona, offers green space, a pool, and a lake, making it a perfect place for relaxation and leisure. Open until 10:30 PM.

Civic Space Park

Address: 424 N Central Ave, Phoenix, AZ
This park in Phoenix, Arizona, features modern sculptures and open spaces for the public to enjoy. It's a great place to experience the city's contemporary art scene. Open until 11 PM.

Desert Breeze Park

Address: 660 North Desert Breeze Blvd E, Chandler, AZ
Desert Breeze Park in Chandler, Arizona, offers a lake and sports areas for various outdoor activities. A fantastic location for family fun and sports enthusiasts. Open until 10:30 PM.

Desert Foothills Park

Address: 1010 E Marketplace Wy SW, Phoenix, AZ
Desert Foothills Park provides open spaces for leisure and outdoor activities in Phoenix, Arizona. It's an excellent spot for an evening stroll or a daytime picnic. Open until 11 PM.

Desert Mountain Park

Address: 22201 Hawes Rd, Queen Creek, AZ

Desert Mountain Park in Queen Creek, Arizona, features playgrounds and fields, catering to families and sports lovers. Open until 10 PM.

Discovery District Park

Address: 2214 E Pecos Rd, Gilbert, AZ

Located in Gilbert, Arizona, Discovery District Park offers soccer fields and playgrounds, making it an ideal location for sports and family activities. Open until 10 PM.

Dreamy Draw Recreation Area

Address: 2421 E Northern Ave, Phoenix, AZ

Dreamy Draw Recreation Area offers hiking and biking trails for outdoor enthusiasts in Phoenix, Arizona. It's a perfect escape for those seeking adventure and natural beauty. Open until 11 PM.

Echo Canyon Recreation Area

Address: 4925 E McDonald Dr, Phoenix, AZ

Echo Canyon Recreation Area offers scenic hiking trails and breathtaking views, providing an ideal setting for outdoor enthusiasts looking to explore the natural beauty of Phoenix.

Eldorado Park

Address: 2311 N Miller Rd, Scottsdale, AZ

Eldorado Park serves as a vibrant recreation hub in Scottsdale, featuring ample amenities for leisure and activities. Open until 10:30 PM.

Encanto Park

Address: 2605 N 15th Ave, Phoenix, AZ

Encanto Park is a serene retreat in Phoenix offering golf, fishing, and scenic views, making it a perfect escape within the city. Open until 11 PM.

Enchanted Island Amusement Park

Address: 1202 W Encanto Blvd, Phoenix, AZ

Enjoy a day of fun with family at Enchanted Island Amusement Park, featuring rides and pedal boats for all ages. Open until 8 PM.

Estrella Mountain Regional Park

Address: 14805 W Vineyard Ave, Goodyear, AZ

Explore the diverse landscapes of desert and wetlands at Estrella Mountain Regional Park, a haven for nature lovers. Open until 8 PM.

Estrella Star Tower

Address: Estrella Pkwy, Goodyear, AZ

Visit Estrella Star Tower for an immersive experience in observation and nature in Goodyear. Open until 8:15 PM.

Freestone District Park

Address: 1045 E Juniper Ave, Gilbert, AZ

Freestone District Park offers various sports facilities and play areas, ideal for family outings and sports enthusiasts. Open until 10 PM.

Frontier Town

Address: 6245 E Cave Creek Rd, Cave Creek, AZ

Step back in time at Frontier Town, a Western-themed park offering a unique glimpse into the Wild West. Open until 5 PM.

Friendship Park

Address: 12325 W McDowell Rd, Avondale, AZ
Friendship Park is a community-centered space in Avondale, perfect for sports and social gatherings. Open until 10 PM.

Granada Park

Address: 6505 N 20th St, Phoenix, AZ
Granada Park provides a recreational space for leisure and activities in Phoenix. Open until 10 PM.

Hurricane Harbor Phoenix

Address: 4243 W Pinnacle Peak Rd, Glendale, AZ
Cool off and enjoy thrilling water rides at Hurricane Harbor Phoenix, the ultimate destination for water park fun. Open until 5 PM.

Lake Pleasant

Address: 41835 N Castle Hot Springs Rd, Morristown, AZ
Lake Pleasant Regional Park is a vast outdoor area ideal for water activities like boating, fishing, and water skiing, as well as camping and hiking. A great destination for those looking to enjoy water sports and the scenic desert landscape.

Manistee Ranch

Address: 5127 W Northern Ave, Glendale, AZ
Explore the historical Manistee Ranch in Glendale, a snapshot of local heritage and history. Open until 8 PM.

McCormick-Stillman Railroad Park

Address: 7301 E Indian Bend Rd, Scottsdale, AZ
Enjoy train rides and playgrounds at McCormick-Stillman Railroad Park, perfect for family outings. Open until 6 PM.

Mesa Grande Cultural Park

Address: 1000 N Date, Mesa, AZ
Discover Native American ruins and learn about Arizona's indigenous cultures at Mesa Grande Cultural Park. Open until 4 PM.

Phoenix Bat Cave

Address: 3698-3694 E Colter St, Phoenix, AZ
Experience natural wildlife viewing at the Phoenix Bat Cave, a unique urban wildlife site. Open 24 hours.

Phoenix Mountains Preserve

Address: 2701 Piestewa Peak Dr, Phoenix, AZ
Engage in urban hiking and explore the natural landscapes of Phoenix Mountains Preserve. Open until 7 PM.

Piestewa Peak Park

Address: 2701 Piestewa Peak Dr, Phoenix, AZ
Tackle the hiking trails of Piestewa Peak Park for breathtaking views and a rewarding workout. Open until 7 PM.

Pioneer Park

Address: 526 E Main St, Mesa, AZ
Enjoy recreational and sports activities at Pioneer Park, a community hub in Mesa. Open until 10 PM.

Pinnacle Peak Park

Address: 26802 N 102nd Way, Scottsdale, AZ

Challenge yourself with hiking and climbing adventures at Pinnacle Peak Park. Open until 5:30 PM.

Red Mountain Park

Address: 7745 E Brown Rd, Mesa, AZ

Engage in a variety of outdoor activities at Red Mountain Park, a versatile recreation area. Open until 10 PM.

Riparian Preserve at Water Ranch

Address: 2757 E Guadalupe Rd, Gilbert, AZ

Explore nature and water conservation efforts at Riparian Preserve at Water Ranch. Open until 10 PM.

Riverview Park

Address: 2100 W Rio Salado Pkwy, Mesa, AZ

Discover climbing and splash pad fun at Riverview Park, ideal for families and children. Open now.

Sahuaro Ranch Park

Address: 9802 59th Ave, Glendale, AZ

Visit Sahuaro Ranch Park for a mix of historical sites and natural beauty. Open until 10 PM.

San Tan Mountain Regional Park

Address: 6533 W Phillips Rd, Queen Creek, AZ

Experience the natural desert terrain and outdoor activities at San Tan Mountain Regional Park. Open until 8 PM.

Scottsdale Xeriscape Garden

Address: 5401 Hayden Rd, Scottsdale, AZ

Learn about water conservation and desert landscaping at Scottsdale Xeriscape Garden. Open until 10 PM.

Hole in the Rock

Address: 625 N Galvin Pkwy, Phoenix

Discover the unique natural geological formation, Hole in the Rock, offering great hiking opportunities and an iconic view of the Phoenix skyline.

Desert Botanical Garden

Address: 1201 N Galvin Pkwy, Phoenix, AZ
Explore the Desert Botanical Garden, a living museum home to over 50,000 desert plants displayed in beautifully designed outdoor exhibits. A must-visit to appreciate the beauty and diversity of desert flora. Open until 8 PM.
Website: www.dbg.org

The Japanese Friendship Garden of Phoenix

Address: 1125 N 3rd Ave, Phoenix, AZ
Experience tranquility at the Japanese Friendship Garden of Phoenix, a traditional Japanese stroll garden featuring a serene koi pond. A peaceful escape offering a scenic and contemplative experience. Open Tuesday – Sunday, 9AM - 4 PM.
Closed on Monday
Website: www.japanesefriendshipgarden.org

Dobbins Lookout

Address: Piestewa Peak Dr, Phoenix, AZ
Visit Dobbins Lookout for breathtaking panoramic views from one of the highest points in the city. Ideal for photography enthusiasts and sightseeing. Open until 7 PM

Margaret T. Hance Park

Address: 67 W Culver St, Phoenix, AZ
Enjoy leisure and picnics at Margaret T. Hance Park, a central urban green space hosting the Japanese Friendship Garden among other amenities. A perfect spot for relaxation and cultural exploration in the heart of Phoenix. Open until 10:30 PM.

Urban Attractions and Activities
Downtown Glendale

Description: Located on West Glendale Avenue, this district features a charming blend of historic brick buildings and modern shops, restaurants, and entertainment venues.
Ambiance: Offers a mix of historical charm and modern development, with a focus on family-friendly activities.
Activities: Explore unique shops, enjoy diverse dining options, catch a movie at the Harkins Theatre Glendale 16, or attend events at the Gila River Arena or the Glendale Historic District. **Website:** https://visitdowntownglendale.com/

Description: Situated along 1 West Rio Salado Parkway, this district is a lively hub known for its college town atmosphere, vibrant nightlife, and diverse entertainment options.

Ambiance: Offers a bustling and energetic atmosphere with a strong presence of Arizona State University students.

Activities: Explore eclectic shops, discover unique restaurants, enjoy live music at various venues, or take a walk or bike ride along the scenic Tempe Town Lake.

Website: https://www.downtowntempe.com/go/downtown-tempe-community

Similarities:

- Both districts offer a variety of shopping and dining options.
- Both are easily accessible and have ample parking.
- Both districts hold events throughout the year.

Accommodation Options

Downtown Phoenix

Hyatt Regency Phoenix

Address: 122 N 2nd St, Phoenix, AZ 85004

Website: https://www.hyatt.com/

Description: This towering hotel provides contemporary accommodations, featuring a rooftop bar-and-grill with stunning city views, a spacious atrium, and a refreshing outdoor pool.

Price: Rates start from $258 per night.

Cambria Hotel Downtown Phoenix Convention Center

Address: 222 E Portland St, Phoenix, AZ 85004

Website: https://www.choicehotels.com/arizona/phoenix

Description: A trendy and relaxed setting awaits in this stylish hotel, featuring a vibrant rooftop bar, a state-of-the-art gym, and a lively restaurant.

Price: Starting from $259 per night.

Hotel San Carlos

Address: 202 N Central Ave, Phoenix, AZ 85004

Website: https://www.sancarlosphoenix.top/

Description: Dive into history at this classic hotel, operational since 1928, providing timeless rooms, complimentary internet, and a scenic rooftop pool.

Price: Rates begin at $137 per night.

The Clarendon Hotel and Spa (21+ Only)

Address: 401 W Clarendon Ave, Phoenix, AZ 85013

Website: https://www.goclarendon.com/

Description: An adults-only hotel offering chic accommodations with a rooftop deck, an authentic Mexican restaurant, a relaxing spa, and an inviting outdoor pool.

Price: Starting from $259 per night.

FOUND:RE Phoenix Hotel
Address: 1100 N Central Ave, Phoenix, AZ 85004
Website: https://www.foundrehotels.com/
Description: Immerse yourself in the arts at this boutique hotel, where inspiration and comfort blend seamlessly in the vibrant downtown setting.
Price: Starting from $490 per night.

Kimpton Hotel Palomar Phoenix
Address: 2 E Jefferson St, Phoenix, AZ 85004
Website: https://www.hotelpalomar-phoenix.com/
Description: Luxuriate in the upscale ambiance, with sophisticated rooms and premium amenities, ensuring an unforgettable stay in the heart of Phoenix.
Price: Starting from $400 per night.

Egyptian Motor Hotel BW Signature Collection
Address: 765 Grand Ave, Phoenix, AZ 85007
Website: https://www.egyptianmotorhotel.com/
Description: A retro-chic hotel offering a lively ambiance and trendy rooms, centrally located for easy access to local attractions and dining.
Price: Starting from $250 per night.

Drury Inn & Suites Phoenix Airport
Address: 3333 E University Dr, Phoenix, AZ 85034
Website: https://www.druryhotels.com/
Description: Perfect for travelers seeking proximity to the airport, this hotel offers comfortable rooms, complimentary hot breakfast, and an evening kickback with free hot food and cold beverages.
Price: Starting from $300 per night.

Scottsdale

Scottsdale Camelback Resort
Address: 6302 E Camelback Rd, Scottsdale, AZ 85251
Website: http://www.scottsdalecamelback.com
Description: A distinguished 4-star condo resort featuring a spa, restaurant, golf course, and hot tub, nestled in the serene landscapes of Scottsdale. Ideal for a rejuvenating retreat with luxurious amenities.
Features: Spa, Pool, Golf course, Hot tub.

The Scottsdale Plaza Resort & Villas
Address: 7200 N Scottsdale Rd, Paradise Valley, AZ 85253
Website: https://www.scottsdaleplaza.com
Description: This sprawling 4-star hotel, conference center, and spa offers a lavish Scottsdale experience with its extensive amenities and elegant design, perfect for both leisure and business.
Features: Spa, Pool, Hot tub, Free Wi-Fi.

Hotel Valley Ho
Address: 6850 E Main St, Scottsdale, AZ 85251
Website: https://www.hotelvalleyho.com/
Description: Indulge in the posh ambiance of this 4-star mid-century modern hotel, complete with a spa, pool, and air-conditioned comfort for a stylish stay in Scottsdale.
Features: Spa, Pool, Hot tub, Air-conditioned.

Kasa Scottsdale Quarter Phoenix
Address: 15235 N 73rd St, Scottsdale, AZ 85254
Website: https://kasa.com/
Description: Experience modern luxury at Kasa Scottsdale Quarter Phoenix, offering exquisite amenities including a pool and golf course for an unforgettable stay.
Features: Pool, Golf course, Free Wi-Fi, Free parking.

Sonesta ES Suites Scottsdale Paradise Valley
Address: 6040 N Scottsdale Rd, Scottsdale, AZ 85253
Website: https://www.sonesta.com
Description: A modern 3-star extended-stay hotel that provides a comfortable and contemporary setting complete with a pool and hot tub, designed for longer visits.
Features: Pool, Hot tub, Free Wi-Fi, Air-conditioned.

Comfort Suites Scottsdale @ Talking Stick
Address: 9215 E Hummingbird Ln, Scottsdale, AZ 85250
Website: https://www.choicehotels.com/arizona
Description: This informal all-suite 2-star hotel is known for its welcoming atmosphere, pool, and complimentary breakfast, catering to guests looking for value and comfort.
Features: Pool, Golf course, Hot tub, Free breakfast.

Sonesta Suites Scottsdale Gainey Ranch
Address: 7300 E Gainey Suites Dr, Scottsdale, AZ 85258
Website: https://www.sonesta.com
Description: An upscale 3-star all-suite hotel offering lush poolside relaxation and top-tier amenities, making for an elegant Scottsdale stay.
Features: Pool, Hot tub, Free Wi-Fi, Free parking.

Aiden By Best Western Scottsdale North
Address: 10801 N 89th Pl, Scottsdale, AZ 85260
Website: https://www.bestwestern.com
Description: A 3-star casual hotel providing a relaxed Scottsdale experience with its pool, dining options, and convenient location, suitable for all types of travelers.
Features: Pool, Golf course, Hot tub, Free Wi-Fi.

Bespoke Inn Scottsdale
Address: 3701 N Marshall Way, Scottsdale, AZ 85251
Website: http://bespokeinnscottsdale.com/
Description: This 4-star boutique lodging offers a unique and intimate stay in Scottsdale, complete with complimentary bikes to explore the city's charm.
Features: Boutique atmosphere, Bikes available for guests.

Tempe

Element Scottsdale at SkySong
Address: 1345 N Scottsdale Rd, Scottsdale, AZ 85257
Website: https://www.marriott.com/
Description: Experience relaxation at this laid-back 3-star hotel, which boasts modern dining options, a refreshing pool, and well-appointed rooms. Ideal for travelers seeking a blend of comfort and convenience.
Features: Pool, Free breakfast, Free Wi-Fi, Air-conditioned.

Residence Inn by Marriott Tempe Downtown/University
Address: 510 S Forest Ave, Tempe, AZ 85281
Description: An informal extended-stay 3-star hotel offering a welcoming atmosphere with a pool, hot tub, complimentary breakfast, and spacious accommodations tailored for longer stays.
Features: Pool, Hot tub, Free breakfast, Free Wi-Fi.

Drury Inn & Suites Phoenix Airport
Address: 3333 E University Dr, Phoenix, AZ 85034
Website: https://www.druryhotels.com/
Description: A casual 3-star airport hotel providing a comfortable stay with amenities such as a pool, free parking, hot tub, and complimentary breakfast, making it perfect for transit travelers.
Features: Pool, Free parking, Hot tub, Free breakfast.

Omni Tempe Hotel at ASU
Address: 7 E University Dr, Tempe, AZ 85281
Website: https://www.omnihotels.com/
Description: This 4-star hotel offers luxurious accommodations with a pool, providing a serene escape and convenient amenities, nestled near Arizona State University for both leisure and business travelers.
Features: Pool, Free Wi-Fi, Air-conditioned, Breakfast.

Homewood Suites by Hilton Phoenix Airport South
Address: 4750 E Cotton Center Blvd, Phoenix, AZ 85040
Description: Enjoy the comforts of home at this 3-star extended-stay hotel, which features spacious suites, a pool, and complimentary shuttle service, catering to guests looking for a homely experience.
Features: Pool, Free parking, Hot tub, Free breakfast.

Fairfield Inn & Suites by Marriott Phoenix Tempe/Airport
Address: 2222 S Priest Dr, Tempe, AZ 85282
Description: This modern 2-star hotel provides an enjoyable stay with its outdoor pool, contemporary rooms, and excellent service, ensuring a relaxed and refreshing visit.
Features: Pool, Free parking, Hot tub, Free breakfast.

Staybridge Suites Phoenix - Chandler, an IHG Hotel
Address: 3990 W Chandler Blvd, Chandler, AZ 85226
Description: A relaxed 3-star hotel offering comfortable accommodations with a pool, gym, and the convenience of a fully equipped kitchen in every suite, suited for both short and long-term stays.
Features: Pool, Free parking, Hot tub, Free breakfast.

Hilton Garden Inn Phoenix/Tempe ASU Area
Address: 86 S Rockford Dr, Tempe, AZ 85281
Description: An all-suite 3-star hotel featuring an outdoor pool and comprehensive amenities, offering a comfortable and convenient base for visitors to the ASU area.
Features: Pool, Free parking, Free Wi-Fi, Air-conditioned.

Glendale

The Wigwam
Address: 300 E Wigwam Blvd, Litchfield Park, AZ 85340
Description: Experience grandeur and tranquility at this luxurious resort offering a seamless blend of history, elegance, and recreation with multiple dining options, championship golf courses, and a signature spa.
Features: Pool, Spa, Free parking, Hot tub
Website: www.wigwamarizona.com

Comfort Suites Glendale - State Farm Stadium Area
Address: 9824 W Camelback Rd, Glendale, AZ 85305
Description: A convenient stay awaits at this comfortable hotel, offering complimentary breakfast and Wi-Fi, perfect for travelers visiting the State Farm Stadium Area.
Website: www.choicehotels.com/arizona

GreenTree Hotel Phoenix West
Address: 1500 N 51st Ave, Phoenix, AZ 85043
Description: Sit back and relax in this straightforward hotel featuring essential amenities for a comfortable stay including a pool and on-site dining.
Features: Pool, Free parking, Hot tub, Free breakfast
Website: www.greentreeinn.com/hotels/az/phoenix-west

Holiday Inn Express Peoria North - Glendale, an IHG Hotel
Address: 16771 N 84th Ave, Peoria, AZ 85382
Description: Experience comfort and convenience with modern amenities and an inviting outdoor pool at this well-located hotel.
Features: Pool, Free parking, Free breakfast, Free Wi-Fi | **Website:** www.ihg.com

TownePlace Suites by Marriott Phoenix Glendale Sports & Entertainment District
Address: 7271 N Zanjero Blvd, Glendale, AZ 85305
Description: Feel at home in this all-suite hotel, offering spacious accommodations and convenient amenities close to Glendale's entertainment options.
Features: Pool, Hot tub, Free breakfast, Free Wi-Fi
Website: www.marriott.com

La Quinta Inn & Suites by Wyndham Phoenix I-10 West
Address: 4929 W McDowell Rd, Phoenix, AZ 85035
Description: Enjoy the essential comforts of home in a convenient location with complimentary Wi-Fi and breakfast served daily.
Features: Free parking, Hot tub, Free breakfast
Website: www.wyndhamhotels.com

Sonesta Simply Suites Phoenix Glendale
Address: 11411 N Black Canyon Hwy, Phoenix, AZ 85029
Description: Discover affordable comfort and convenience, ideal for both short and extended stays, with an outdoor pool and well-appointed suites.
Features: Pool, Hot tub, Free Wi-Fi, Air-conditioned
Website: www.sonesta.com

Drury Inn & Suites Phoenix Happy Valley
Address: 2335 W Pinnacle Peak Rd, Phoenix, AZ 85027
Description: Enjoy exceptional value and comfort, complemented by free hot breakfast, evening snacks, and a welcoming atmosphere.
Features: Pool, Free parking, Hot tub, Free breakfast
Website: www.druryhotels.com

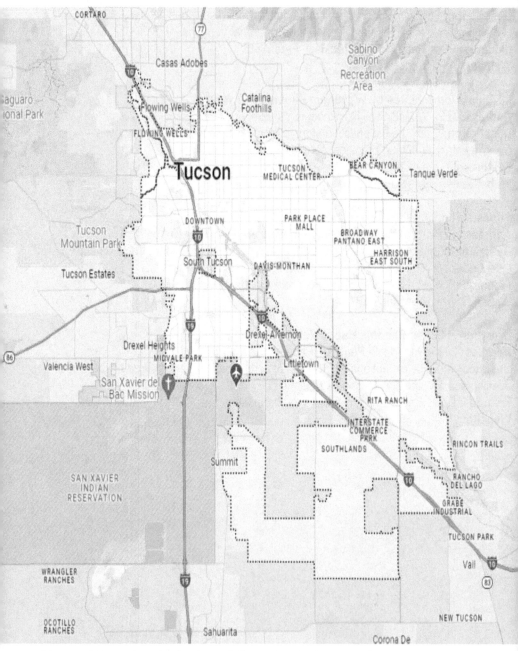

Tucson, Arizona, is a city that beautifully marries its rich cultural heritage with the stunning natural beauty of the Sonoran Desert. Known for its vibrant history, diverse arts scene, and culinary delights, Tucson offers a unique Southwestern experience.

The list below includes a wide range of tourist attractions located in Tucson and the surrounding vicinity.

Arizona-Sonora Desert Museum

Location: 2021 N Kinney Rd, Tucson, AZ 85743

Description: This unique destination in Tucson transcends the traditional museum experience, combining elements of a zoo, botanical gardens, and an interactive museum. Engage in an educational journey as you explore walking trails adorned with diverse plant species. Enjoy encounters with native Arizona wildlife, including ocelots, wolves, and snakes. Enhance your visit with staff-led interactions, where you can meet owls up close and learn about their habitats. Don't miss the raptor free flight show at 10 am,

showcasing birds like ravens, owls, and falcons in an impressive display of natural behavior.

Amenities: On-site dining options include a restaurant and a snack shop offering hot sandwiches and salads. The gift shop presents a selection of unique items perfect for souvenirs.

Visitor Tip: Allocate a few hours to fully experience all the museum has to offer. Located near the entrance to Saguaro National Park West, it's an excellent addition to any Tucson itinerary.

Opening Hours: Daily, until 5 PM | **Website:** www.desertmuseum.org

The Mini Time Machine Museum of Miniatures

Location: 4455 E Camp Lowell Dr, Tucson, AZ 85712

Description: Discover a captivating world in miniature at this unique museum, dedicated to the art of miniature houses and scenes. The exhibits range from intricate modern

creations to historical pieces from the 17th and 18th centuries, each displaying remarkable craftsmanship and attention to detail. Visitors are encouraged to take their time to appreciate the nuances of each display and the stories they tell.

Visitor Tip: Prepare for more than one visit to fully appreciate the intricate details of each exhibit. Photos capture hidden details not immediately apparent, revealing more with each glance.

Opening Hours: Daily, until 4 PM, Closed on Monday

Website: www.theminitimemachine.org

Highly recommended for an enchanting journey through time and imagination, perfect for all ages.

Tucson Botanical Gardens

Location: 2150 N Alvernon Way, Tucson, AZ 85712

Description: Explore the serene beauty of the Tucson Botanical Gardens, spanning over five acres filled with a diverse range of plants and a captivating butterfly house. Wander through the lush landscapes that seem larger than life, with meticulously labeled flora that educates as well as enchants. Delve into the distinct sections of the garden, including an impressive assortment of cacti and a fascinating collection of African aloes, showcasing the adaptive beauty of succulents from around the world. A highlight is the Washed Ashore art exhibit, combining art with environmental conservation, showcasing sculptures made from ocean debris.

Opening Hours: Daily, until 4:30 PM

Website: www.tucsonbotanical.org

Pima Air & Space Museum

Location: 6000 E Valencia Rd, Tucson, AZ 85756

Description: An expansive museum that offers a comprehensive look at aviation history with a vast collection of aircraft spanning military, private, and international origins. Engage in a journey of discovery and inspiration, experiencing the grandeur of aviation, from historical legends to modern marvels. The outdoor displays are extensive, so visiting during cooler months allows for a more comfortable exploration of the museum's outdoor components.

Visitor Tip: Allocate a full day for your visit, especially if including the highly recommended Tram tour. Dress appropriately for outdoor exploration, especially during cooler months.

Opening Hours: Daily, until 5PM

Website: www.pimaair.org

Old Tucson

Location: 201 Kinney Rd, Tucson, AZ 85735

Description: Old Tucson offers a unique blend of Hollywood history and family fun set against the backdrop of the Arizona desert. Originally built in 1939 as a film set, this iconic location has hosted some of the greatest names in Western cinema. Today, it operates as a family theme park, providing a rich, immersive Western experience. Visitors can enjoy live shows, stagecoach and train rides, and interact with characters that bring the Old West back to life.

Features: Live entertainment, historical tours, rides, and seasonal events in a setting that has been a part of Hollywood's Western film history.

Visitor Tip: Allocate a full day to explore all the attractions and shows. The park offers a mix of entertainment and education that appeals to both adults and children.

Opening Hours: Generally open 10 AM to 5 PM, with Tuesdays closing at 4 PM

Website: http://oldtucson.com/

Reid Park Zoo

Location: 3400 E Zoo Ct, Tucson, AZ 85716

Description: Nestled in the heart of Tucson, Reid Park Zoo spans 24 acres and offers a friendly, interactive zoo experience. Ideal for family outings, this compact zoo allows visitors to comfortably explore various habitats within a day. The zoo prides itself on the well-being and care of its animals, offering a close-up view of exotic and native wildlife, including the adorable baby giraffe and vibrant flamingos.

Features: Interactive exhibits, easy navigation, family-friendly atmosphere, diverse animal encounters, and special children's area.

Visitor Tip: Plan a two-hour visit to fully enjoy all the exhibits without rushing. Memberships offer great value for frequent visitors.

Opening Hours: 9 AM to 4 PM on weekdays, extending to 6 PM on weekends

Website: https://reidparkzoo.org/

Tucson Rodeo Parade Museum

Address: 4823 S 6th Ave, Tucson, AZ 85714

Description: This museum offers a deep dive into the rich history of the Tucson Rodeo Parade, one of the city's signature events, featuring an array of historical artifacts, local heritage items, and a vast collection of horse-drawn carriages. It's not just about the rodeo; it's a comprehensive journey through Tucson's past.

Visiting Hours: Open Thursday, Friday, Monday, Tuesday, and Wednesday from 8 AM to 4 PM; closed on Saturday and Sunday.

Website: https://www.tucsonrodeoparade.com/the-museum/

Saguaro National Park

Location: Various entrances around Tucson, AZ; main visitor centers are located at 2700 N. Kinney Road, Tucson, AZ 85743 (West District) and 3693 S. Old Spanish Trail, Tucson, AZ 85730 (East District).

Description: Saguaro National Park is an iconic American national park that celebrates the life and landscape of the Sonoran Desert. Here, the majestic Saguaro cacti, a symbol of the American West, stand tall amid a varied backdrop of desert flora and fauna. The park offers a unique opportunity to explore the vast and vibrant ecosystem home to an incredible diversity of wildlife, from black bears and bobcats to a myriad of bird species.

Activities: Visitors can enjoy a range of outdoor activities such as hiking on various trails, picnicking amidst nature, wildlife viewing, and educational tours. The park's two districts, the Rincon Mountain District (East) and the Tucson Mountain District (West), offer different experiences and landscapes, from the more developed trails and historical areas in the West to the quieter, flatter terrains suitable for biking and leisurely walks in the East.

Visitor Tips: The best times to visit are during the cooler months from October to April. Be sure to participate in the guided tours available at the visitor centers to learn about the park's biodiversity. Don't forget to carry water, sunscreen, and appropriate outdoor gear to enhance your desert adventure.

Opening Hours: 9 AM – 5 PM daily

Website: https://www.nps.gov/sagu/index.htm

Location: 140 N Main Ave, Tucson, AZ 85701

Description: Located in the heart of Tucson, the Tucson Museum of Art is a cultural haven showcasing a diverse range of art exhibits. The museum complex features a rich collection of contemporary, Southwestern, and Latino art, offering visitors an insightful look into the region's artistic heritage.

Highlights: Explore the permanent collections, enjoy the rotating special exhibits, and stroll through the serene outdoor sculpture garden. A notable highlight is the impressive collection of Indigenous artists located on the lower level near the shop.

Opening Hours: Wednesday to Sunday, 10 AM – 5 PM; Closed Mondays and Tuesdays

Website: http://www.tucsonmuseumofart.org/

Sabino Canyon Recreation Area

Address: 5700 N Sabino Canyon Rd, Tucson, AZ 85750

Description: Sabino Canyon is a natural paradise located in Tucson, Arizona, offering visitors a chance to explore the rugged canyons and lush desert landscapes of the Coronado National Forest. This recreation area is famous for its scenic vistas, flowing streams, and a diverse ecosystem that includes towering saguaro cacti and various wildlife. The area caters to outdoor enthusiasts of all levels, providing a multitude of hiking and camping options.

Activities: Hikers can choose from a variety of trails that range from easy walks to challenging treks. The Sabino Canyon tram offers a narrated tour of the canyon, allowing visitors to learn about the area's natural history while enjoying the stunning scenery. For $15 per person, with kids under 3 riding free, the tram ride is a great option for families or those who wish to explore deeper into the canyon without a strenuous hike.

Visitor Tips: Parking at Sabino Canyon requires a fee of $8 per vehicle, but entry is free with a National Park pass. Arrive early to secure parking and avoid the hotter parts of the day, especially during the summer months. Spring visits offer the unique opportunity to see the desert in bloom and streams filled with water from winter rains.

Opening Hours: Open 24 hours, but tram and visitor center hours may vary.

Tumamoc Hill

Address: Tumamoc Hill Rd, Tucson, AZ 85745
Description: Tumamoc Hill stands as a landmark in Tucson, Arizona, offering both locals and visitors a unique blend of physical challenge and natural beauty. This 860-acre ecological reserve is not only a hub for scientific research but also a protected area showcasing the rich biodiversity of the Sonoran Desert.
Activities: The 3-mile round-trip hike on Tumamoc Hill is a popular activity for fitness

enthusiasts and nature lovers alike. The paved trail, with an elevation gain of 700 feet, provides a moderately challenging trek suitable for all fitness levels. Along the way, hikers can explore ruins, view educational markers in both Spanish and English, and enjoy panoramic views of the Tucson area. An audio tour available for download enhances the experience.
Visitor Tips: The best times for hiking are during the cooler parts of the day or at sunset, especially during the monsoon season when the skies are dramatic, and rainbows are common. Though the trail has benches, they are mostly in the sun, so carrying water and wearing sun protection is advisable. Porta potties and a water refilling station are located near the start of the trail. Parking can be tight, so arriving early or during off-peak hours is recommended. While street parking is considered safe, it's wise to secure your belongings to prevent theft.
Opening Hours: Open until 10 PM daily. | **Website:** http://tumamoc.arizona.edu/

Presidio San Agustin del Tucson Museum

Location: 196 N Court Ave, Tucson, AZ 85701
Insight: Nestled in the heart of Tucson, the Presidio San Agustin del Tucson Museum is a time capsule inviting visitors to explore Tucson's layered history. From ancient indigenous cultures to Spanish, Mexican, and early American periods, this fort museum is a testimony to the city's multifaceted past.
Experience: Begin your visit with a delightful coffee from the nearby Dandelion Cafe before wandering through the museum's exhibits. Inside, you'll find meticulously preserved architecture and artifacts that narrate Tucson's story before and after Spanish colonization. Outside, the museum expands into the original Presidio area, offering a tangible connection to history.
Visitor Tips: Dedicate enough time to meander both the indoor and outdoor sections. If

possible, align your visit with the cannon firing schedule for a unique historical reenactment. Enjoy the serene ambiance of the outdoor Presidio grounds after exploring the indoor narratives.
Operational Hours: Open from Wednesday to Sunday, 10 AM to 4 PM. Closed on Mondays and Tuesdays. **More Information:** Visit http://www.tucsonpresidio.com/ for additional details, events, and visitor guidelines.

Flandrau Science Center and Planetarium

Location: 1601 E University Blvd, Tucson, AZ 85721

Insight: Located within the University of Arizona, the Flandrau Science Center and Planetarium is a gateway to the stars and much more. Catering to space enthusiasts and curious minds, this destination blends education with entertainment through its extensive exhibits and captivating planetarium shows.

Highlights: The Tucson Skies presentation offers a beginner-friendly overview of astronomy, while the laser light shows bring a vibrant twist to the planetarium experience. Whether you're a family, a solo explorer, or on a unique date, the center provides a cool respite from the Arizona heat and a fascinating educational experience.

Visitor Tips: Ensure you explore both floors; the lower level's interactive space might be easy to miss. The venue is suitable for all ages, with educational games and activities that appeal to both children and adults. Plan your visit to coincide with one of the scheduled laser light shows for an unforgettable experience.

Operational Hours: Open from Wednesday to Sunday, 10 AM to 5 PM. Closed on Mondays and Tuesdays.

Admission Fees: Adult entry ranges from $21 to $30.

More Information: For details on showtimes, exhibits, and special events, visit https://flandrau.org/

Children's Museum Tucson

Location: 200 S 6th Ave, Tucson, AZ 85701

Overview: The Children's Museum Tucson stands as a beacon of creativity and educational play in the heart of the city. It's a vibrant space where children of all ages can dive into hands-on activities, stimulating their curiosity and love for learning in a fun-filled environment.

Experiences: From interactive exhibits to daily creative activities, the museum offers a plethora of opportunities for kids to explore, create, and discover. Each corner of the museum is designed with the young mind in mind, ensuring that every visit is both educational and entertaining.

Community Commitment: Admission is kept affordable, with special initiatives in place to ensure that all families, regardless of income, can enjoy what the museum has to offer. This inclusivity is a testament to the museum's dedication to the community.

Visitor Tips: Plan your visit during weekdays for a more intimate experience with less crowd. Explore the outdoor areas before heading inside for the full range of exhibits. Take advantage of the educational opportunities and be sure to interact with the friendly staff who are there to enhance your experience.

Operational Hours: Open Wednesday to Sunday, 9 AM to 5 PM, with extended hours till 7 PM on Thursdays. Closed on Mondays.

More Information: Dive into the world of interactive learning and check out upcoming events by visiting https://www.childrensmuseumtucson.org/ .

Arizona State Museum

Location: 1013 E University Blvd, Tucson, AZ 85721

Overview: Located within the University of Arizona campus, the Arizona State Museum is a cultural gem dedicated to preserving the rich heritage of the American Southwest. It

...tands as an educational sanctuary, offering in-depth insights into regional anthropology, archaeology, and indigenous cultures.

Exhibitions: Engage with a variety of exhibits showcasing Native American artifacts, historical pottery collections, and fascinating archaeological finds. Each display is meticulously curated to educate and inspire visitors about the deep-rooted history and traditions of the region.

Visiting Hours: The museum welcomes visitors from Wednesday to Saturday, 10 AM to 4 PM, providing ample opportunity to explore its extensive collections and learn from its informative displays.

Further Information: To plan your visit and discover more about the museum's current exhibitions and special events, please visit https://statemuseum.arizona.edu/visit .

Trail Dust Town

Location: 6541 E Tanque Verde Rd, Tucson, AZ 85715

Overview: Trail Dust Town offers a unique Old West experience, perfect for family outings and history enthusiasts alike. This Western-themed attraction is filled with vintage charm, providing an immersive glimpse into the past with its collection of historic buildings and period attractions.

Attractions: Visitors can enjoy a variety of activities, from watching live stunt shows that capture the spirit of the Wild West to taking a ride on the miniature train. Although it's free to wander around the town, some attractions may require a small fee, offering good value for a fun experience.

Operating Hours: The town comes to life from Thursday to Sunday, 5 PM to 9 PM, making it an ideal destination for an evening out.

More Details: To learn more about Trail Dust Town's attractions and seasonal events, visit http://www.traildusttown.com/

Arizona History Museum

Address: 949 E 2nd St, Tucson, AZ 85719

Description: Dedicated to exploring the diverse and rich history of Southern Arizona, this museum offers interactive and immersive exhibits. From the early Native American cultures to Spanish colonial artifacts, mining, and the state's evolution, there's something for everyone, making it a must-visit for history buffs and families alike.

Visiting Hours: Open from 10 AM to 3 PM on Thursday, Friday, Tuesday, and Wednesday; closed on Saturday, Sunday, and Monday.

Website: http://www.arizonahistoricalsociety.org/

Will You Escape?

Address: 2577 N 1st Ave, Tucson, AZ 85719

Description: Challenge yourself and your friends at "Will You Escape?", Tucson's thrilling escape room adventure. Experience engaging themes like "Santa's Naughty List," "Serial Killer," and "Witching Hour." Suitable for all ages, this attraction provides a unique and interactive group activity that tests your problem-solving skills in a fun and exciting way.

Visiting Hours: Wednesday to Friday from 1:30 PM to 9 PM; Saturday and Sunday from 11 AM to 9 PM; Monday and Tuesday from 5:30 PM to 9 PM.

Website: http://www.willyouescape.com/

Address: 414 N Toole Ave, Tucson, AZ 85705

Description: Immerse yourself in the rich railroad heritage of So uthern Arizona at this museum located in the historic depot. Explore a variety of exhibits, artifacts, and the famous steam engine No. 1673, featured in the film "Oklahoma!" and listed on the National Register of Historic Places. Ideal for train enthusiasts and history buffs alike.

Visiting Hours: Wednesday, Thursday, and Tuesday from 11 AM to 3 PM; Friday and Saturday from 10 AM to 4 PM; Sunday from 11 AM to 3 PM; Closed on Monday.

Website: http://tucsonhistoricdepot.org/

Titan Missile Museum

Address: 1580 W Duval Mine Rd, Green Valley, AZ 85614

Description: Delve into the chilling history of the Cold War at the Titan Missile Museum, a former missile silo turned into an educational exhibit. Explore the complexities of nuclear weapons and the realities faced by military crews on duty. The museum provides a stark reminder of the nuclear age, offering guided tours that in clude the control room and the missile itself.

Visiting Hours: Open daily from 9:45 AM to 5 PM.

Website: http://www.titanmissilemuseum.org/

San Xavier del Bac Mission

Address: 1950 W San Xavier Rd, Tucson, AZ 85746
Description: Discover the awe-inspiring San Xavier del Bac Mission, a historic landmark established in the late 1700s. This iconic mission showcases spectacular carvings, frescoes, and Moorish architectural influences. Visitors can immerse themselves in the profound history and spiritual ambiance of this well-preserved site. The mission's exterior garden and gift shop offer additional experiences, including local crafts and foods like authentic Mexican burritos and fry bread.
Hours: Open daily until 4 PM. | **Website:** http://www.sanxaviermission.org/

Javelina Rocks

Address: Cactus Forest Dr, Tucson, AZ 85748
Description: Javelina Rocks, located within the scenic bounds of Tucson, offers a natural escape where visitors can explore and climb distinctive rock formations. Approximately two-thirds into Cactus Forest Drive, this spot provides convenient parking and access to breathtaking 360-degree views of the surrounding desert and mountain ranges. Ideal for photography, hiking, or simply enjoying the serene desert landscape, Javelina Rocks is a must-visit for nature lovers and outdoor enthusiasts.
Hours: Open daily until 5 PM.

University of Arizona Museum of Art

Address: 1031 N Olive Rd, Tucson, AZ 85721
Description: The University of Arizona Museum of Art is a cultural gem, offering an expansive collection that spans from the Renaissance to the 20th century. This two-story museum presents both permanent and visiting exhibitions, beautifully curated to showcase a variety of art styles. From war-themed pieces and religious depictions to abstract and modern art, there's something to appeal to all tastes. With a peaceful courtyard and outdoor sculptures, it's a haven for art enthusiasts.
Hours: Wednesday to Saturday from 10 AM to 4:30 PM, closed on Sundays and Mondays. | **Website:** http://artmuseum.arizona.edu/

Jácome Plaza

Type: City Park
Address: 101 N Stone Ave, Tucson, AZ 85701
Description: Nestled in the bustling heart of downtown Tucson, Jácome Plaza is a hub of urban vitality and cultural exchange. This lively city park is renowned for hosting prominent events such as the electrifying DUSK Music Festival and the culturally rich Tucson Meet Yourself Folklife Festival. Here, community, culture, and entertainment intertwine, offering visitors an array of experiences from multi-stage music performances to diverse culinary delights, including unique treats like Freeze Dried Candy. Committed to maintaining a welcoming and secure environment, the plaza is upheld by dedicated volunteers, ensuring a pleasant visit for both locals and tourists. **Opening Hours:** Open daily until 10:30 PM.
Upcoming Events:

- DUSK Music Festival: November 9-10, 2024
- Tucson Meet Yourself Folklife Festival: October 4-6, 2024

Tucson Desert Art Museum and Four Corners Gallery

Address: 7000 E Tanque Verde Rd, Tucson, AZ 85715
Description: The Tucson Desert Art Museum is a hidden gem that showcases a unique collection of Hopi textiles, Navajo weaving, and various artifacts, providing a colorful window into the culture and history of the region. The museum's intimate setting allows for a personal exploration of its beautiful exhibitions, including historical photographs, traditional and modern paintings, and local artists' works.
Hours: Wednesday to Saturday from 10 AM to 4 PM, closed Sunday to Tuesday.
Website: http://www.tucsondart.org/

Tucson Jewish Museum & Holocaust Center

Address: 564 S Stone Ave, Tucson, AZ 85701
Description: Housed within a historic synagogue, the Tucson Jewish Museum & Holocaust Center is a poignant and educational site. Visitors can delve into the rich history of the Jewish community in the Southwest, understanding their significant contributions to Tucson's growth and the diverse culture of the West.
Hours: Wednesday to Sunday from 1 PM to 5 PM, closed on Mondays and Tuesdays.
Website: http://tjmhc.org/

Rio Vista Natural Resource Park

Address: 3974 N Tucson Blvd, Tucson, AZ 85716
Description: Discover the tranquility and natural beauty of Rio Vista Natural Resource Park, a hidden gem at the northern end of Tucson. Situated along the south shore of the Rialito, the park offers breathtaking views of the Catalina Mountains, especially during sunset. Visitors can enjoy a leisurely stroll around the park's walkways, relax at picnic tables, and immerse themselves in the surrounding nature. It's a perfect spot for dog lovers, nature enthusiasts, and anyone looking to enjoy a peaceful outdoor escape.
Hours: Open daily until 10:30 PM.

Rincon Mountain Visitor Center

Address: 3693 S Old Spanish Trail, Tucson, AZ 85730
Description: Start your journey into the heart of the desert at the Rincon Mountain Visitor Center. Perfectly nestled along the scenic 8-mile loop road, this center provides access to a variety of trails, from wheelchair-accessible paths to more challenging hikes. Marvel at the panoramic vistas, discover diverse flora and fauna, and enjoy the serene beauty of the desert landscape.
Hours: Open daily until 5 PM. | **Website:** https://www.nps.gov/sagu/index.htm

Old Pueblo Archaeology Center

Address: 2201 W 44th St, Tucson, AZ 85713
Description: Old Pueblo Archaeology Center is dedicated to preserving and educating about the rich archaeological heritage of the region. The center offers a variety of programs, tours, and exhibits aimed at promoting understanding and appreciation of prehistoric and historic cultures.
Website: http://www.oldpueblo.org/

Kitt Peak National Observatory

Address: Arizona 85735

Description: Kitt Peak National Observatory stands as a hub for astronomical research and stargazing, home to some of the most advanced research telescopes in the world. Visitors can indulge in nightly stargazing events, where the wonders of the universe come alive under expert guidance. By day, the observatory offers educational tours showcasing the science and technology behind the study of the cosmos. Whether you're an avid astronomer or a curious tourist, Kitt Peak provides a unique opportunity to look beyond our planet and explore the depths of space.

Hours: Wednesday, Thursday, Monday, and Tuesday from 9 AM to 5 PM; Friday to Sunday from 9 AM to 4 PM.

Website: https://kpno.noirlab.edu/

Picture Rock Petroglyphs

Address: 7301 W Picture Rocks Rd, Tucson, AZ 85743

Description: Picture Rock Petroglyphs is an open-air gallery of ancient art etched into the desert varnish of the Tucson area. This timeless attraction is accessible 24 hours, inviting visitors to wander and wonder at the symbols and stories carved by indigenous peoples centuries ago. The site offers not just a glimpse into the artistic expression of the past but also a serene desert landscape that has inspired generations. Perfect for history buffs, nature lovers, and cultural explorers, the Picture Rock Petroglyphs provide a silent yet profound narrative of the area's ancient inhabitants.

Carnival of Illusion

Address: 160 S Scott Ave, Tucson, AZ 85701

Description: Carnival of Illusion offers a captivating blend of illusion and comedy in an intimate setting, making it a unique entertainment experience in Tucson. Limited to around 60 guests per show, this magical performance engages audiences with interactive acts, ensuring a personal and unforgettable experience. Perfect for a unique evening out, the show is family-friendly but best suited for children aged 10 and up due to the length and format. Attendees contribute to a noble cause, as proceeds aid in the restoration of the historic Scottish Rite building.

Hours: Wednesday, Thursday, Tuesday from 9 AM to 10 PM, Friday, and Saturday from 9 AM to 10 PM.

Website: https://www.carnivalofillusion.com/

The University of Arizona Alfie Norville Gem & Mineral Museum

Address: 115 N Church Ave Ste 121, Tucson, AZ 85701

Description: This museum showcases a stunning array of mineral specimens, meteorites, and gems, making it a haven for geology and gem enthusiasts. The collection includes beautifully preserved stones, sparkling gems, and ancient fossils, providing visitors with an informative and visually appealing experience. Whether you're a seasoned mineralogist or simply intrigued by natural history, the museum offers a unique educational journey through the earth's geological wonders.

Hours: Thursday to Wednesday from 10 AM to 4 PM, closed on Sundays and Mondays.

Website: https://gemandmineralmuseum.arizona.edu/

Valley of the Moon

Address: 2544 E Allen Rd, Tucson, AZ 85716
Description: Step into the whimsical world of
Valley of the Moon, a fantasy-themed park
designed to kindle imagination and wonder.
With its history of promoting kindness and
imagination, this enchanting garden is a haven
for storytelling, magic, and exploration.
Suitable for visitors of all ages, it captivates
both the yo ung and the young at heart with its
tales of fairies, trolls, and other mystical
beings.
Hours: Check the website for current event
times and openings.
Website: http://www.tucsonvalleyofthemoon.com/

Fort Lowell Museum

Address: 2900 N Craycroft Rd, Tucson, AZ 85712
Description: Delve into the rich history of U.S. cavalry and Native American heritage at
the Fort Lowell Museum. Located in the remains of the historic Fort Lowell, this museum
provides a glimpse into the brief yet significant Civil War history in Arizona. Visitors can
explore quaint exhibits displaying artifacts and learn about the life and times at the fort.
The museum offers an intimate look at the area's past, from military life to Native
American history, making it a worthwhile visit for history buffs and casual visitors alike.
Hours: Thursday to Saturday from 9 AM to 2 PM, closed Sunday through Wednesday.
Website: https://tucsonpresidio.com/fort-lowell/

Ignite Sign Art Museum

Address: 331 S Olsen Ave, Tucson, AZ 85719
Description: Explore the vibrant world of neon at the Ignite Sign Art Museum, a colorful
and educational homage to the art of sign-making and neon design. Founded in 2018, this
family-run museum displays a vast collection of historical and artistic signs, offering
visitors an immersive journey through the evolution of sign art. Engage in interactive
displays, participate in a scavenger hunt, and witness live neon bending demonstrations.
The museum's unique collection and interactive exhibits make it a must-visit destination
for art lovers and history enthusiasts alike.
Hours: Wednesday to Saturday from 10 AM to 4 PM, closed Sunday through Tuesday.
Website: http://www.ignitemuseum.com/

Colossal Cave Mountain Park

Address: 16721 E Old Spanish Trail, Vail, AZ 85641
Description: Colossal Cave Mountain Park is known for its extensive cave system and
beautiful desert landscape. The park offers guided cave tours, including the standard tour
and more adventurous options like ladder and wild tours, providing an exciting and
educational experience for visitors of all ages.
Website: http://www.colossalcave.com/

Red Hills Visitor Center

Address: 2700 N Kinney Rd, Tucson, AZ 85743

Description: Located in the heart of Saguaro National Park, the Red Hills Visitor Center offers guided hikes, educational programs, and maps to explore the surrounding desert. It's an excellent starting point for visitors looking to learn about the unique ecosystem of the Sonoran Desert and the majestic Saguaro cacti.

Website: http://www.nps.gov/sagu/index.htm

Museum of Contemporary Art Tucson

Address: 265 S Church Ave, Tucson, AZ 85701

Description: Discover the cutting-edge side of Tucson's art scene at the Museum of Contemporary Art. Housed in a spacious venue, the museum presents seasonal exhibitions showcasing a blend of local and international artists. The exhibitions often touch on poignant themes, such as immigration and community, reflecting the region's cultural and social landscape. Enjoy innovative art in a dynamic setting, making the most of MOCA's small but impactful space, especially during the Free Third Thursdays events.

Hours: Thursday to Saturday from 11 AM to 6 PM, Sunday from 11 AM to 4 PM, closed Monday through Wednesday.

Website: http://www.moca-tucson.org/

Mission Garden

Address: 946 W Mission Ln, Tucson, AZ 85745

Description: Mission Garden is a living agricultural museum that reconstructs Tucson's Spanish Colonial walled garden tradition. Explore various garden plots from different time periods and cultures, including Native American, Spanish Colonial, Mexican, and Territorial gardens.

Website: http://www.missiongarden.org/

Opening Hours: Wednesday to Saturday, 8 AM – 2 PM; Closed Sunday to Tuesday.

390th Memorial Museum

Address: 6000 E Valencia Rd, Tucson, AZ 85756

Description: This museum is a tribute to the brave men of the 390th Bombardment Group who served during World War II. Visitors can explore the extensive collection, including a meticulously restored B-17 bomber, and learn about the lives and sacrifices of these young servicemen.

Website: http://www.390th.org/ | **Opening Hours:** Daily, 10 AM – 4:30 PM

DeGrazia Gallery in the Sun

Address: 6300 N Swan Rd, Tucson, AZ 85718

Description: This iconic gallery is dedicated to showcasing the diverse artwork of Ted DeGrazia, set against the beautiful backdrop of Tucson's mountain ranges. Visitors can explore a variety of mediums, including mosaics, sketches, paintings, and pottery, all housed within DeGrazia's original adobe architecture.

Website: http://degrazia.org/

Opening Hours: Open daily until 4 PM; a must-visit for art lovers and cultural explorers visiting Tucson.

Franklin Auto Museum

Address: 1405 E Kleindale Rd, Tucson, AZ 85719
Description: The Franklin Auto Museum showcases a remarkable collection of Franklin automobiles and memorabilia, celebrating the innovation and history of the H.H. Franklin Company. Car enthusiasts and history buffs alike will find the museum's exhibits and classic car collections fascinating.
Website: https://franklinmuseum.org/
Opening Hours: Thursday to Saturday, 10 AM – 4 PM; Closed Sunday to Wednesday

Desert Discovery Nature Trail

Location: Tucson, AZ 85743
Description: This short, accessible, paved loop trail offers a quick but thorough exploration of the Sonoran Desert environment. With informative panels along the way, visitors can learn about the diverse types of cacti and other desert plants, making it an educational walk for all ages. Ideal for photography, especially during the golden hour, and provides an easy, educational outing.
Opening Hours: Open 24 hours

Tin Town

Address: 357 N Tyndall Ave, Tucson, AZ 85719
Phone: +15208693470
Description: Tin Town is a hidden gem in Tucson, offering an immersive experience into a recreated western town. Visitors can enjoy a unique stay in the saloon-themed Airbnb, surrounded by meticulously collected historical artifacts and craftsmanship that narrate a rich local history. Ideal for history enthusiasts and those looking for a distinctive accommodation option.
Visitor's Note: Advance booking is recommended to ensure a guided tour and a complete experience of this labor of love.

Yume Japanese Gardens of Tucson

Address: 2130 N Alvernon Way, Tucson, AZ 85712
Description: This tranquil and beautifully designed garden offers a slice of Japanese serenity and aesthetics in Tucson. Visitors can explore the thoughtfully arranged landscapes, a ceremonial tea room, and a variety of plants and structures that evoke the calm and beauty of traditional Japanese gardens. The site is perfect for those looking to find peace and quiet amidst the city's hustle and bustle.
Website: http://www.yumegardens.org/
Opening Hours: Thursday to Saturday from 9:30 AM to 4:30 PM, Sunday from 12 PM to 5 PM.

Steam Pump Ranch

Address: 10901 N Oracle Rd, Oro Valley, AZ 85737
Description: Located in the picturesque Oro Valley, Steam Pump Ranch offers visitors a glimpse into Arizona's ranching history. While primarily known for its Saturday morning farmers market, the ranch also features the historic Pusch House exhibit, providing insights into the life and times of the 1880s. Although it's a smaller market, it offers quality

products and a chance to experience local culture and history. The site also plays an active role in raising awareness for important social issues such as human trafficking.
Website: https://www.orovalleyaz.gov/
Opening Hours: Saturdays from 8 AM to 12 PM.

Linda Vista Trail

Address: 730 E Linda Vista Rd, Oro Valley, AZ 85737
Description: The Linda Vista Trail offers an enjoyable outdoor experience suitable for the entire family. This trail provides options ranging from an easy stroll to more challenging mountain ascents. Visitors of all skill levels can find a path that suits their adventure level. The trail is well-maintained, featuring dirt paths with intriguing rock steps and a manageable incline. Opting for the loop starting clockwise from the entrance, hikers can enjoy about a two-mile trek, generally completed in under an hour. Parking is available in a small lot near the trailhead, with additional overflow parking across the street. The surrounding area offers breathtaking natural beauty, making it an ideal choice for a day hike. **Opening Hours:** Open daily until 9 PM.

Anamax Recreation Center | Anamax Park - Town of Sahuarita

Address: 17501 S Camino De Las Quintas, Sahuarita, AZ 85629
Description: Anamax Recreation Center, nestled within Anamax Park, provides a family-friendly environment with ample facilities for sports and recreational activities. The center itself is modest yet well-maintained, offering a range of classes, including sewing, with ample space for participants. The surrounding park caters to a variety of interests, boasting a skate ramp, outdoor exercise equipment, a walking path, and a playground among other amenities. The basketball courts, large fields with lights, and picturesque picnic areas make it a beloved community hub. The playground, particularly suited for younger children, is safely fenced, ensuring a relaxed atmosphere for parents and guardians.
Opening Hours: Open daily until 5 PM.
Website: http://sahuaritaaz.gov/Index.aspx?NID=197

Gadsden-Pacific Division Toy Train Operating Museum

Address: 3975 N Miller Ave, Tucson, AZ 85705
Description: Discover a world of enchantment at the Gadsden-Pacific Division Toy Train Operating Museum, a premier destination for model train enthusiasts and families alike. Recognized as a favorite among model train museums nationwide, this unique museum captivates visitors with its passionate volunteers and interactive displays. Guests can engage with the exhibits by pressing buttons to animate the scenes, following trains along their tracks, and delving into the rich history behind each model. Learn the tales of trains' origins and their first conductors, adding depth to every chug and whistle. Outside, experience the joy of a miniature train ride, journeying through a quaint western town, or take the controls of the larger model trains for a hands-on adventure. Whether you're a lifelong train aficionado or new to the hobby, a visit to this museum promises a fascinating, fun-filled day for visitors of all ages.
Opening Hours: Sunday 1–4 PM. Closed Monday to Saturday.
Website: https://gadsdenpacific.org/

Sweetwater Preserve Trailhead

Address: 4001 N Tortolita Rd, Tucson, AZ 85745

Description: A haven for hikers and nature lovers, Sweetwater Preserve Trailhead offers an array of well-marked trails, ensuring visitors can explore without fear of losing their way. Ideal for sunset hikes, the area provides stunning panoramic views and an array of trail options suitable for varying skill levels. The Wildflower Ridge Trail and part of the Desperado Loop are particularly popular for their scenic beauty and tranquility, allowing visitors to immerse themselves in the serene desert landscape.

Website: http://pima.gov/

Opening Hours: Open daily until 5 PM.

Tucson Audubon Society

Address: 300 E University Blvd #120, Tucson, AZ 85705

Description: A must-visit for bird enthusiasts and nature lovers, the Tucson Audubon Society offers a welcoming and informative environment. The on-site store provides a range of gifts ideal for nature aficionados, alongside expert advice for attracting and observing birds. Visitors can also test various binoculars to find the perfect match for their birdwatching needs. Membership offers added benefits like discounts, supporting the society's conservation efforts. The staff is knowledgeable and ready to assist with all bird-related inquiries.

Website: http://tucsonaudubon.org/

Opening Hours: Thursday to Friday from 10 AM to 4 PM, Saturday from 10 AM to 2 PM.

Philabaum Glass Gallery

Address: 711 S 6th Ave, Tucson, AZ 85701

Description: Philabaum Glass Gallery is a premier destination for those interested in contemporary glass art. This gallery and studio feature an excellent selection of works from a variety of artists, showcasing diverse styles and techniques. Visitors can expect to find unique pieces of molded glass art, among other exquisite forms. The staff at Philabaum are praised for their knowledge and friendliness, enhancing the overall visitor experience. The gallery offers reasonable prices for those looking to purchase a memorable piece of art.

Opening Hours: Thursday to Saturday from 10 AM to 4 PM; Closed Sunday to Wednesday. | **Website:** http://www.philabaumglass.com/

ASARCO Mineral Discovery Center & Mine Tours

Address: 1421 W Pima Mine Rd, Sahuarita, AZ 85629

Description: The ASARCO Mineral Discovery Center provides a fascinating glimpse into the world of mining with scheduled guided mine tours. The scale of the operation is astonishing, with an emphasis on modern automation, showcasing a significantly reduced human workforce despite full operational status. This unexpected find offers visitors an enlightening experience on the complexities of mining. The tour guides, while still gaining familiarity with their roles, are equipped with reference documents ensuring they provide accurate and engaging information.

Opening Hours: Thursday to Sunday from 9 AM to 5 PM; Closed Monday and Tuesday.

Website: https://www.asarco.com/discoverycenter/

Fantasy Island Mountain Bike Park (North)

Address: 9500 E Irvington Rd, Tucson, AZ 85730
Description: Fantasy Island Mountain Bike Park offers a range of trails suitable for various skill levels, from advanced beginners to intermediates. The park is celebrated for its well-maintained trails, varying terrains, and scenic views, enhancing the biking experience. Signage and trail cues are appreciated for aiding navigation, though more signage at intersections could improve the experience. The park provides a mix of challenge and fun, with different entrance points catering to different skill levels. It's a perfect escape into nature, offering trails like Bunny loop for a short ride or combining it with Bunny's Revenge and Snake for a longer adventure. Remember, desert tires or tire treatment is essential due to sandy spots along the trails.
Opening Hours: Open 24 hours.

Windy Point Vista

Address: 930 Catalina Hwy, Mt Lemmon, AZ 85619
Description: Windy Point Vista provides breathtaking views comparable to the famous Cabot Trail's Skyline Trail. It's a perfect scenic stop on your journey up or down Mount Lemmon, offering free access to expansive vistas. The area is pet-friendly and offers a range of trails for various skill levels. Early morning visits offer a serene experience, enhanced by the area's natural beauty. Be cautious on the rocky outlooks as there are no safety rails. The location is a popular gathering spot for motorcycle enthusiasts, so parking may vary depending on the time and day. Facilities include public restrooms, and the area is accessible 24 hours, allowing for flexible visitation.
Opening Hours: Open 24 hours.

Molino Canyon Vista

Address: General Hitchcock Hwy, Tucson, AZ 85749
Description: Molino Canyon Vista offers visitors tranquil scenery and the potential for beautiful waterfalls, though availability can vary with the weather conditions. While water levels might be lower during dry seasons, the scenic beauty and serenity of the canyon remain undiminished. The area is ideal for visitors seeking peace and natural beauty, with impressive rock formations and mountains that echo the quiet majesty of the surroundings. Recommended for visits at sunrise for a peaceful and awe-inspiring start to the day. Note that waterfalls are more likely after rains, so plan accordingly for the best experience.
Opening Hours: Accessible at all times, but best visited during daylight for safety and visibility.

Postal History Foundation Inc

Address: 920 N 1st Ave The, Tucson, AZ 85719
Description: The Postal History Foundation Inc in Tucson offers a unique glimpse into the fascinating world of postal and philatelic history. This charming small museum captivates visitors with its array of displays and exhibits, showcasing a rich collection of stamps, covers, and postcards. The experience is enhanced by the friendly staff and their resident dog, making it a warm and welcoming visit. Ideal for history enthusiasts and casual visitors alike, this attraction provides a delightful educational experience free of charge. Ensure to

check the museum's schedule to avoid coinciding with school field trips for a more personal visit.

Opening Hours: Monday, Tuesday, Wednesday, Thursday, and Friday from 8:30 AM to 2:30 PM. Closed on Saturday and Sunday.

Website: http://postalhistoryfoundation.org/

Seven Falls

Type: Hiking Area

Address: 5700 N Sabino Canyon Rd, Tucson, AZ 85750

Description: Seven Falls is a hiker's paradise located within the Sabino Canyon area, known for its scenic trails leading to a series of beautiful waterfalls. This outdoor adventure spans approximately 7-8 miles round-trip and is both rewarding and relaxing, offering a chance to immerse in the tranquility of nature. Visitors are reminded to come prepared with ample water, sun protection, and suitable hiking footwear to tackle the Arizona sun and rugged terrain.

Opening Hours: Open 24 hours

Oro Valley Archery Range

Type: Tourist Attraction

Address: 660 W Naranja Dr, Oro Valley, AZ 85737

Description: The Oro Valley Archery Range is a top-notch facility catering to archery enthusiasts of all levels, from beginners to experienced archers. This well-maintained range offers two walkable 3D courses, and a range with targets from 10 to 100 yards, providing varied challenges for all. With a small fee per shooter or the option for a yearly pass, it's an accessible spot for individuals and families alike. The Oro Valley community and visitors enjoy the inclusive, family-friendly environment, making it an excellent activity for all ages. **Opening Hours:** Open daily until 6 PM

Website: https://www.orovalleyaz.gov

Parks and Nature

Agua Caliente Regional Park

Address: 12325 E Roger Rd, Tucson, AZ 85749

Description: Agua Caliente Regional Park offers visitors a peaceful escape into nature's serene beauty, with its well-maintained paths winding through lush landscapes, punctuated by hot springs and abundant wildlife. Ideal for family outings, the park is a sanctuary where children and adults alike can enjoy the presence of local ducks and engage with the natural environment. With clean facilities and ample parking, even during busier times, it's a perfect spot for picnics, leisurely walks, or simply soaking in the tranquil surroundings. | **Website:** https://www.pima.gov/1244/Agua-Caliente-Park

Lincoln Regional Park

Address: 4325 S Pantano Rd, Tucson, AZ 85730

Description: Lincoln Regional Park is a diverse desert regional park and sports complex located in Tucson, Arizona. This vast park provides numerous recreational activities and facilities, including basketball courts, a children's playground, and a splash pad. With extensive open hours, the park offers ample time for visitors to enjoy various outdoor activities. **Opening Hours:** Daily from 6 AM to 10:30 PM

Sweetwater Wetlands Park

Address: 2511 W Sweetwater Dr, Tucson, AZ 85745

Description: Sweetwater Wetlands Park is an urban wildlife habitat and birding spot, providing a lush green oasis in the desert city of Tucson. This park is known for its abundant water features and diverse vegetation, creating a perfect habitat for a wide range of bird species. Easy-to-navigate trails allow visitors to explore the area thoroughly, offering a peaceful retreat from city life. The park's tranquil environment and the soothing sounds of nature make it an ideal spot for relaxation and wildlife observation. **Website:** https://www.tucsonaz.gov/

John F. Kennedy Park

Address: 3700 S Mission Rd, Tucson, AZ 85713

Description: John F. Kennedy Park is a sprawling outdoor space in Tucson featuring areas for picnicking, fishing, and children's play. This large park caters to a variety of recreational needs and is a great spot for community gatherings, outdoor activities, and relaxation. With its sizable lake, families can enjoy fishing or simply bask in the natural surroundings. **Opening Hours:** Open daily until 10:30 PM

Brandi Fenton Memorial Park

Address: 3482 E River Rd, Tucson, AZ 85718

Description: Brandi Fenton Memorial Park is a vibrant and family-friendly park located in Tucson, Arizona. This park offers a wide range of recreational facilities including a splash pad, equestrian arena, and various sports fields. It's a perfect destination for family outings, offering ample space for picnics, sports, and leisure activities. The park is well-maintained and provides a safe, enjoyable environment for visitors of all ages. **Opening Hours:** Open daily until 10 PM

Address: 221 E Wetmore Rd, Tucson, AZ 85705

Description: Funtasticks Family Fun Park provides a plethora of family-friendly attractions and activities. From go-karts a nd laser tag to mini-golf, a ropes course, and a water park, there's something for everyone to enjoy. While some areas may need updating, the park offers a great value for a day's entertainment without breaking the bank. Birthday party packages are available, enhancing the fun for special occasions. Despite some areas for improvement, the park's variety of attractions and friendly staff make it a fun day out for families.

Opening Hours: Varies by day; typically 12 PM to 8 PM on weekdays and 10 AM to 10 PM on weekends

Website: http://www.funtasticks.com/

Christopher Columbus Park

Address: 4300 N Silverbell Rd, Tucson, AZ 85745

Description: Christopher Columbus Park is a diverse outdoor area offering a variety of recreational activities. Known for its spacious environment and scenic views, the park is ideal for those seeking a peaceful day out in nature. With facilities to cater to different interests, it's a well-loved spot among locals and visitors alike.

Opening Hours: Open daily until 10:30 PM

Kennedy Park

Address: 3357 S La Cholla Blvd, Tucson, AZ 85713

Description: Kennedy Park offers a blend of natural beauty and recreational spaces, ideal for family outings and social gatherings. Featuring well-maintained facilities and a welcoming atmosphere, it's a popular destination for both leisure and activity. The park ensures a fun-filled day for visitors with its diverse amenities.

Opening Hours: Open daily until 10:30 PM

Chuck Ford Lakeside Park

Address: 8201 E Stella Rd, Tucson, AZ 85730

Description: Chuck Ford Lakeside Park is a picturesque family-friendly park known for its cleanliness and natural beauty. The park offers a peaceful trail for walking, vast grassy areas for picnics, and a children's playground. Ducks roam freely by the lake, adding to the serene environment. While swimming is not permitted, fishing and relaxing by the lake make for a perfect day out.

Opening Hours: Open daily until 10:30 PM

Armory Park

Address: 222 S 5th Ave, Tucson, AZ
Description: Armory Park, nestled in the heart of Tucson, provides a tranquil setting with its well-maintained paths and lush greenery. This historic park also houses a senior center and offers various community-focused activities. It's a great spot for leisurely walks, family gatherings, and outdoor relaxation.
Opening Hours: Open daily until 10 PM

Tucson Mountain Park

Address: 8451 W McCain Loop, Tucson, AZ 85735
Description: Tucson Mountain Park is a sprawling natural reserve offering an abundance of trails for hiking and biking. The park is home to the Gilbert Ray Campground, noted for its spacious and well-maintained sites. Visitors can enjoy the vast landscapes, local wildlife, and outdoor activities like archery in this expansive park.
Website: https://www.pima.gov/1272/Tucson-Mountain-Park

Canada del Oro Riverfront Park

Address: 551 W Lambert Ln, Oro Valley, AZ 85737
Description: Situated in Oro Valley, Canada del Oro Riverfront Park is a well-loved community space offering various recreational facilities. The park's open spaces, sports fields, and scenic views make it a favorite among locals for sports, picnics, and leisurely strolls.
Opening Hours: Open daily until 10 PM | http://www.orovalleyaz.gov/parksandrec

Himmel Park

Address: 1000 N Tucson Blvd, Tucson, AZ
Description: Himmel Park is a vibrant neighborhood park that offers a variety of recreational opportunities including a swimming pool, tennis courts, and playgrounds. It's a hub of activity and relaxation, perfect for community members of all ages.
Opening Hours: Open daily until 10:30 PM

Gene C. Reid Park

Address: 900 S Randolph Way, Tucson, AZ 85716
Description: Gene C. Reid Park is a sprawling green oasis in the city, featuring a dog park, duck pond, and ample space for various outdoor activities. It's a popular destination for both locals and tourists looking for a natural escape within the urban landscape.
Opening Hours: Open daily until 10:30 PM

Case Natural Resource Park

Address: 9815 E Kenyon Dr, Tucson, AZ 85748
Description: Case Natural Resource Park is a serene and expansive area perfect for nature lovers and outdoor enthusiasts. The park offers ample space for leisurely walks, picnics, and bird watching.
Opening Hours: Open daily until 7 PM

Arthur Pack Regional Park

Address: 9101 N Thornydale Rd, Tucson, AZ 85742
Description: Arthur Pack Regional Park is a multifaceted park featuring a dog park, soccer fields, and walking paths. It is well-equipped with sheltered picnic areas and clean restrooms, making it an ideal spot for family outings and recreational sports.
Opening Hours: Open daily until 6 PM

Palo Verde Park

Address: 425 S Mann Ave, Tucson, AZ
Description: Palo Verde Park is a community hub offering a variety of outdoor activities. The park is perfect for evening strolls, family picnics, and recreational sports, boasting well-maintained grounds and ample space for everyone.
Opening Hours: Open daily until 10:30 PM

Colossal Cave Mountain Park

Address: 16721 E Old Spanish Trail, Vail, AZ 85641
Description: Known for its historic cavern tours, Colossal Cave Mountain Park combines adventure with natural beauty. Explore the underground wonder with expert guides and enjoy the park's additional amenities, including equestrian trails and a cozy café.
Website: http://colossalcave.com/

Crossroads at Silverbell District Park

Address: 7548 N Silverbell Rd, Tucson, AZ 85743
Description: This park is a family-friendly destination featuring a fun splash pad, well-maintained bike trails, and children's playgrounds. Located adjacent to the library, it offers a perfect blend of education and recreation.
Website: http://www.maranaaz.gov/parks/

Thomas Jay Regional Park

Address: 6465 S Craycroft Rd, Tucson, AZ
Description: A well-rounded park offering various recreational options, Thomas Jay Regional Park is renowned for its beauty and family-friendly amenities. Whether for sports, picnics, or playgrounds, there's something here for everyone.
Opening Hours: Open daily until 10 PM

Pima Prickly Park

Address: 3500 W River Rd, Tucson, AZ
Description: An eco-friendly project turned stunning attraction, Pima Prickly Park showcases a vast array of cacti and desert plants, rescued and transplanted from various construction sites. A peaceful spot to explore Tucson's natural flora.

Oro Valley Parks & Recreation

Address: 10555 N La Cañada Dr, Oro Valley, AZ
Description: Offering diverse fitness and recreational activities, Oro Valley Parks & Recreation is the perfect spot to inject energy and fun into your daily routine. Features include aquatic fitness classes and a vibrant community atmosphere.
Opening Hours: Open daily until 9 PM

Alvernon Park

Address: 701 N Longfellow Ave, Tucson, AZ
Description: Alvernon Park stands out for its ample green spaces and variety of recreational opportunities, complemented by an engaging recreation center, perfect for family outings.
Opening Hours: Open daily until 10:30 PM

Accommodation Options

Luxury Resorts

Loews Ventana Canyon Resort
A high-end resort nestled in the Catalina Foothills, offering luxury amenities, golf courses, and spa services.
Address: 7000 N Resort Dr, Tucson, AZ 85750
Website: https://www.loewshotels.com/ventana-canyon
Contact: +1 520-299-2020

The Westin La Paloma Resort & Spa
A luxurious resort with stunning mountain views, featuring a golf course, spa, and multiple swimming pools.
Address: 3800 E Sunrise Dr, Tucson, AZ 85718

Boutique Hotels and Inns

Arizona Inn:
A historic boutique hotel in a residential area, known for its elegant rooms and gardens.
Address: 2200 E Elm St, Tucson, AZ 85719
Website: https://www.arizonainn.com/

Hotel Congress
A trendy hotel in downtown Tucson, known for its vibrant nightlife and unique style.
Address: 311 E Congress St, Tucson, AZ 85701
Website: https://hotelcongress.com/

Bed and Breakfasts

The Royal Elizabeth Bed & Breakfast:
A cozy, intimate and charming Victorian-style B&B located in downtown Tucson.
Address: 204 S Scott Ave, Tucson, AZ 85701
Website: https://royalelizabeth.com/

Casa Tierra Adobe Bed & Breakfast Inn
A desert retreat offering adobe-style accommodations, set in the tranquil Sonoran Desert.
Address: 11155 W Calle Pima, Tucson, AZ 85743
Website: http://www.casatierra.com/

Budget-Friendly Options

Red Roof Inn Tucson South - Airport:
An affordable and pet-friendly hotel offering comfortable amenities and easy access to the airport.
Address: 3704 E Irvington Rd, Tucson, AZ 85714
https://www.redroof.com/

La Quinta Inn & Suites by Wyndham Tucson Airport:
A budget-friendly hotel near the airport, with an outdoor pool and complimentary breakfast.
Address: 7001 S Tucson Blvd, Tucson, AZ 85756
https://www.wyndhamhotels.com

When searching for luxury accommodations, many travelers turn to trusted online platforms to find the best options tailored to their specific needs and preferences. One of the premier destinations for such accommodations is Marriott, which can be explored via their official website, www.marriott.com. Marriott is renowned for offering a wide range of luxury hotels and resorts worldwide, providing exquisite amenities, exceptional service, and unforgettable experiences. From urban retreats in bustling cities to tranquil beachfront resorts, Marriott caters to every type of luxury traveler.

In addition to Marriott's own platform, www.booking.com is another excellent resource for finding accommodations. This website offers a vast selection of hotels, apartments, and unique stays worldwide, including luxury options. Booking.com is user-friendly, providing detailed descriptions, customer reviews, and photos to help travelers make an informed decision. The platform often features competitive prices and free cancellation options, making it a flexible choice for planning luxury stays.

TripAdvisor is not only a source for hotel reviews but also offers the ability to book accommodations directly through its website (https://www.tripadvisor.com). It stands out for its comprehensive user reviews and ratings, which can be invaluable in choosing the right luxury accommodation. Travelers can read firsthand experiences from other guests before making a booking decision. TripAdvisor also aggregates prices from different booking sites to help find the best deals, ensuring travelers can access luxury accommodations at the best possible price.

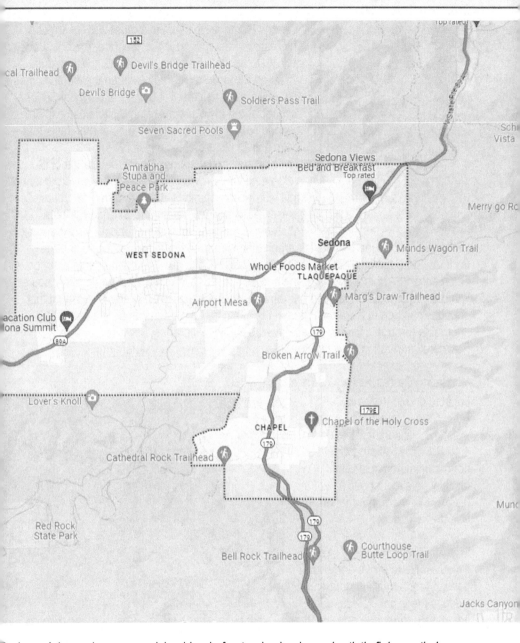

Sedona, Arizona, is a mesmerizing blend of natural splendor and artistic flair, nestled amidst striking red rock formations that have captivated artists, spiritual seekers, and outdoor enthusiasts alike. This small city is renowned for its scenic beauty, thriving arts scene, and a unique sense of tranquility that pervades its atmosphere.

The list below includes a wide range of tourist attractions located in Sedona and the surrounding vicinity.

Sedona Heritage Museum is a must-visit for anyone interested in the rich history of Sedona, Arizona. Located at 735 Jordan Rd, Sedona, AZ 86336, this museum offers an educational journey through the life and times of Sedona's early settlers, including the family of Sedona Schnebly, the town's namesake. Visitors can explore historic buildings filled with antiques and artifacts that paint a vivid picture of local history.

The museum is a testament to the dedication of its volunteers who provide insights into the development of this vibrant community. Celebrating over 25 years of preservation and education, the Sedona Heritage Museum is an ideal destination for both young and old.

Highlights include the original telegraph office featured in the movie "Angel and the Badman," and the opportunity to see native wildlife like quail on the museum grounds. Open from 11 AM to 3 PM daily, the museum is a peaceful place to spend a few hours immersing yourself in the past. For families, the museum offers a scavenger hunt that engages children in the exploration of the exhibits. Admission can be made more affordable through Cultural Passes available at local libraries.

For more information, visit their website: http://www.sedonamuseum.org

Montezuma Castle National Monument

Located on Montezuma Castle Rd in Camp Verde, AZ, welcomes visitors from 8 AM to 4:45 PM daily, offering ample opportunities to explore this fascinating site steeped in history. For more information, visit their website: https://www.nps.gov/moca/. To make the most of your visit, it's advisable to arrive early, as parking tends to fill up quickly. Despite the initial crowds, once you pass through the pay line, there's plenty of space to roam and absorb the marvels of this ancient structure. Be sure to bring water and wear comfortable shoes for your exploration.

Many visitors find Montezuma Castle National Monument to be a bucket list-worthy destination. The experience of walking up to the cliff dwellings and immersing oneself in the rich history is truly unforgettable. While there is a $10 admission fee, it's deemed worthwhile for the chance to witness a National Monument up close.

Conveniently located off Interstate 17 between Phoenix and Sedona, the monument is easily accessible for travelers in the area.

Palatki Heritage Site

The Palatki Heritage Site, nestled in Sedona, AZ 86336, offers enriching experiences for visitors throughout the week. Operating hours range from 9:30 AM to 3 PM, with an exception on Wednesday, closing at noon. Reservations are required and can be made through the provided link: http://www.recreation.gov/ticket/facility/10089352.

This site's ease of access made it suitable for all ages. The hike to the destination is straightforward, rewarding explorers with stunning views and a captivating history lesson. If you're in the area, it's certainly worth your time to visit. However, reaching the site requires crossing a challenging dirt/gravel road for the last 6 miles, leaving your vehicle dusted in clay powder. Despite this, the journey is well worth it, with the opportunity to explore petroglyphs and cave dwellings along the trails.

Tuzigoot National Monument

Address: 25 Tuzigoot Rd, Clarkdale, AZ 86324
Hours: 8 AM – 4:45 PM daily
Description: Tuzigoot National Monument showcases the remarkable ruins and history of the indigenous people who once thrived in the Verde Valley. Visitors can explore the remnants of their wisely built and industrious society, offering valuable learning experiences for both kids and adults. The site is accessible, featuring ramps and stairs that lead to panoramic views. The staff is noted for being friendly and informative, enhancing the visitation experience. National Park members can enter for free, while there is an entrance fee for others. Facilities like bathrooms are maintained in good condition.
Website: https://www.nps.gov/tuzi/index.htm

Arizona Copper Art Museum

Address: 849 Main St, Clarkdale, AZ 86324
Hours: 10 AM – 4:30 PM daily
Description: The Arizona Copper Art Museum is a gem in Clarkdale, offering an extensive collection that tells the story of Arizona's history, geography, and the significant role of copper. The museum, located in the historic Clarkdale high school building, features well-organized exhibits in the old classrooms, providing a unique and insightful experience. It's suitable for all ages, offering a deep dive into copper's cultural and practical applications.
Website: http://www.copperartmuseum.com/

Address: 561 AZ-179, Sedona, AZ 86336
Hours: Open daily from 10 AM to 5:30 PM
Description: Exposures International Gallery of Fine Art is one of Sedona's premier art destinations, featuring an extensive collection from over 100 international artists. Visitors can explore a wide range of artistic expressions, from eclectic art pieces to exquisite sculptures and jewelry. The gallery showcases works by Tesa Michaels among other renowned artists, providing a diverse and high-quality selection. Despite the high price points, the quality of the artwork justifies the cost. Voted No 1 Gallery in Arizona and the best museum in Sedona making this a must-visit location for art lovers in Sedona. **Website**: http://www.exposuresfineart.com/

Sedona Chamber of Commerce - Visitor Center

Address: 331 Forest Rd, Sedona, AZ 86336
Hours: Open daily from 8:30 AM to 5 PM
Description: The Sedona Chamber of Commerce - Visitor Center is the perfect starting point for any visit to Sedona. The center offers a plethora of information about the city, including activities, lodging, dining, and sightseeing tips. The friendly and knowledgeable staff are ready to assist with all inquiries, ensuring visitors can fully enjoy their Sedona experience. Highly recommended for first-time visitors, the center provides essential resources for a memorable stay in this stunning area.
Website: https://www.visitsedona.com

Audrey Headframe Park

Address: 55 Douglas Rd, Jerome, AZ 86331

Description: Audrey Headframe Park is a captivating historical site where visitors can explore the rich mining heritage of Jerome. The park showcases old mining equipment, giving a glimpse into the past life of miners in this region. Its most notable feature is the glass viewing platform over a 1,900-foot mine shaft, offering a unique perspective into the depths where miners once worked. The park  provides educational plaques detailing the history and mechanisms of mining that was pivotal to the area's development. It's an ideal spot for history enthusiasts and those looking to delve into the mining past of Jerome.

Opening Hours: 9 AM – 4:30 PM daily.

Website: https://azstateparks.com/jerome/things-to-do/audrey-headframe

Entertainment and Experience

Verde Canyon Railroad

Address : 300 N Broadway, Clarkdale, AZ 86324

Description: Verde Canyon Railroad offers a once-in-a-lifetime train experience through the breathtaking scenery of the Verde Valley. Each passenger receives a personal charcuterie tray, sparking wine, and bottled water, ensuring a comfortable journey. The ride features captivating narrations on the history and geography of the area, complemented by thematic train songs. Opt for riverside seating for the best views. The outdoor train carts offer an immersive experience with educational commentary. Inside, luxury seating provides ample space and comfort, along with access to a bar in every cart.

Opening Hours: 8 AM – 5 PM daily.

Website: https://verdecanyonrr.com/

Blazin' M Ranch

Address: 1875 Mabery Ranch Rd, Cottonwood, AZ 86326
Description: Blazin' M Ranch provides a classic Western experience with an all-you-can-eat homemade meal featuring tender, fall-off-the-bone ribs and a variety of sides. The evening continues with a captivating live show, offering entertainment for all ages. Arrive early to enjoy the full ranch experience, including axe throwing, mechanical bull riding, and target shooting. The venue is perfect for a fun-filled evening, whether it's a special occasion like Valentine's Day or a casual night out.
Opening Hours: 5 PM – 9 PM, closed on Sundays and Mondays.
Website: http://www.blazinm.com/

Bearcloud Gallery

Address: 390 AZ-89A #1, Sedona, AZ 86336
Description: Bearcloud Gallery showcases an exceptional collection of artwork filled with authenticity, magic, and beauty. Visitors often find themselves drawn into the profound and spiritually moving pieces displayed, with each visit uncovering new intricacies and depths within Bearcloud's creations. The artist's dedication to his craft and the stories told through his art make every piece in the gallery a testament to a larger, interconnected narrative. The gallery offers a unique and immersive experience that goes beyond traditional art viewing, inviting guests to reflect on the artwork's deeper meanings.
Opening Hours: Open daily from 10 AM to 5 PM.
Website: http://www.bearcloudgallery.com/

Sedona Offroad Adventures

Address: 2900 W State Rte 89A, Sedona, AZ 86336
Description: Sedona Offroad Adventures offers a thrilling experience for adventure seekers in Sedona. With their punctual service and clean, private vehicles, guests can explore rugged terrains and breathtaking landscapes. The tours are enriched by the knowledge and passion of guides like Brad and Phil, who share fascinating stories and historical facts. A highlight is the hike for stunning views, but be prepared for the rugged roads and changing temperatures. Despite the initial price concerns, guests find the tours valuable, offering unforgettable memories and picturesque scenery unique to Sedona.
Opening Hours: 7 AM – 7 PM daily.
Website: https://www.sedonaoffroadadventure.com

Guidance Air - Sedona

Address: 1200 Airport Rd, Sedona, AZ 86336
Description: Guidance Air offers exceptional helicopter tours in Sedona, providing guests with a unique aerial perspective of the region's stunning landscapes. The experience is enhanced by knowledgeable pilots like the local who shares insights into Sedona's landmarks, ruins, and challenging hikes. The company ensures that all passengers get a window seat, offering unobstructed views of the natural beauty. Whether opting for their extended flights or a shorter journey, visitors are guaranteed a memorable adventure with breathtaking views, especially when taking off in the early morning.
Opening Hours: 8:30 AM – 5:30 PM daily.
Website: https://www.guidanceair.com/

Address: Sedona, AZ 86336

Description: Seven Sacred Pools is an enchanting natural feature located on the outskirts of Sedona, hidden along a scenic half-mile loop trail. Despite being lesser-known and not prominently marked on maps, this attraction draws visitors with its serene beauty and the mystical atmosphere of the pools, which are especially photogenic. While the name suggests a spiritual significance, the actual experience can vary depending on the season; the pools may not always be filled with water but the surrounding landscape remains striking. The hike to the pools is considered moderate, offering breathtaking views and an opportunity to explore further into a bamboo forest and a hidden waterfall. Note that accessing certain areas like a nearby cave may require a bit of agility due to steep inclines.

Opening Hours: 8 AM – 6 PM daily.

Doe Mountain Trail

Address: Doe Mountain, Sedona, AZ 86336

Description: Doe Mountain Trail is an excellent hiking option for families, offering an accessible and enjoyable outdoor adventure. The trail features easy parking and a manageable path suitable for children, including a series of switchbacks leading to the mesa's top. The ascent provides stunning views, especially of Bear Mountain, and culminates in a breathtaking 360-degree panorama at the summit. The entire hike can be completed in approximately 1.5 to 2 hours, making it an ideal choice for those looking for a shorter trek without sacrificing scenic beauty. The trail is particularly appealing for its well-maintained paths and the chance to walk the entire rim of the mountain, offering diverse perspectives of the surrounding Sedona landscape.

Cathedral Rock

Address: Arizona 86351

Description: Cathedral Rock presents an enthralling hiking experience with its challenging scrambles and steep inclines, making it a favorite among thrill-seeking hikers. The trail demands physical prowess and determination, leading to some of the most spectacular views in the Sedona area. Despite the strenuous climb, the reward at the top is unparalleled, with panoramic views that capture the essence of the region's natural beauty. An early start is recommended to enjoy the tranquility and cooler temperatures. Cathedral Rock is not just a hike; it's an adventure that encapsulates the spirit of Sedona, making it a must-visit for those who appreciate the great outdoors. Remember to wear sturdy shoes and bring ample water, especially during warmer months.

Boynton Pass Vortex

Address: Sedona, AZ 86336

Description: Boynton Pass Vortex offers a serene hiking experience with relatively easy access compared to other Sedona vortex sites. The trail provides breathtaking views while allowing visitors to feel the distinctive energy many believe emanates from the vortex. Remember to bring water, especially during warmer months, as the desert climate can intensify the heat. Although there is a parking fee, the area remains a popular trail, particularly bustling during conventional hours. For a more solitary experience, consider visiting early in the morning or around sunset. The contrast between the vortex's serene energy and the surrounding natural beauty creates a unique and peaceful hiking experience, away from the bustle of the town yet still offering magnificent natural landscapes.

Devil's Bridge

Description: Devil's Bridge offers an unforgettable hiking experience with a trail that features a gradual incline, becoming more challenging as you approach the iconic natural arch. Despite its daunting appearance, the bridge provides solid ground and panoramic views of Sedona's landscapes. Caution is advised, especially after rain, as the path may become slippery, and the final ascent can be steep, particularly for young children or those wary of heights. The trail, about 7 miles round trip, is well-marked and popular among visitors, leading to potential crowding, especially at the bridge itself. Starting the hike early in the morning can help avoid the busiest times. Facilities such as bathrooms are available at the trailhead, adding convenience to your adventure.

Website: https://www.fs.usda.gov/recarea/coconino/recarea/?recid=55292

Submarine Rock

Description: Submarine Rock is a unique hiking destination in Sedona, providing a tranquil wilderness escape, especially during off-peak times like Christmas Day. Although the hike is not lengthy, it offers substantial scenic rewards and a peaceful atmosphere, with minimal disturbances even from private jeep tours that occasionally pass through. Ideal for exploring, camping, and hiking, the area requires visitors to be well-prepared with water during summer and rain gear during winter due to possible flash floods. The rock itself serves as an excellent vantage point, offering a stunning 360-degree view of the surrounding landscape. Whether part of a guided tour or a personal journey, Submarine Rock stands out for its natural beauty and panoramic views.

Airport Loop Trails

Address: Airport Road, Sedona, AZ 86336

Description: The Airport Loop Trail, a jewel among Sedona's array of natural wonders, offers an unforgettable hiking experience that encapsulates the essence of Arizona's scenic beauty. This 3.9-mile moderate trail encircles the Airport Mesa, providing hikers with 360-degree views of Sedona's most iconic landmarks, including Bell Rock, Cathedral Rock, and Courthouse Butte. The trail's beginning is marked by an easy yet rocky path, transitioning into more challenging terrains with steep ascents, narrow cliffside paths, and occasional loose rocks. The most arduous section near the vortex area offers both a challenge and the trail's most breathtaking panoramas. Suitable for a wide range of hikers, the Airport Loop is rated from easy to moderate difficulty.

Despite its accessibility, hikers are advised to wear proper trail shoes and carry water, especially as the trail becomes steeper and more rugged. Parking can be found at the trailhead or the scenic overlook parking area when the lot is full, though spaces are limited and tend to fill quickly throughout the year.

Opening Hours: Open 24 hours. However, it is advisable to hike during daylight hours to safely navigate the trail's varying conditions and to fully appreciate the stunning vistas.

Website: http://www.fs.usda.gov/recarea/coconino/recarea/?recid=71905

Bear Mountain Trail

Address: Bear Mountain trail/Oski approach, Sedona, AZ 86336

Description: Bear Mountain Trail presents a strenuous but rewarding hiking experience in Sedona. Despite its challenges, including a steep climb and minimal shade, the trail offers breathtaking views that are well worth the effort. Hikers should be prepared for a sunny journey, potentially without the need for additional layers. Trail markers can be scarce, so staying vigilant is important to remain on the correct path. The hike is most suitable for those with above-average skills and stamina, and carrying ample water is crucial due to the intense exertion and lack of shade. Proper hiking footwear with good grip is essential to navigate rocky sections safely. The trail is best attempted in dry conditions to avoid slippery rock surfaces. Distinguished by white diamond markers, the trail clearly indicates the summit, ensuring a gratifying conclusion to the hike.

Opening Hours: Daily from 10:30 AM to 4 AM.

Snoopy Rock

Address: Sedona, AZ 86336

Description: Snoopy Rock offers an engaging and versatile hiking experience, starting from a gentle path and escalating to a more challenging scramble to reach the iconic rock formation resembling the beloved cartoon character. This destination is perfect for both adventure-seekers and families, with opportunities to tailor the hike's difficulty to your liking. The area is particularly photogenic, providing vast, stunning 360-degree views of Sedona's landscape, so bringing a wide-angle lens is recommended to capture the full beauty. The hike from Marg's trailhead is notably less crowded, offering a more serene and intimate experience compared to more popular trails like Bell Rock.

Soldier Pass Trailhead

Address: Forest Service 9904 Rd, Sedona, AZ 86336

Description: Soldier Pass Trailhead is renowned for its beautiful scenic views and access to unique natural landmarks, including the Devil's Kitchen sinkhole and the Seven Sacred Pools. This trail offers an easy to moderate hiking experience, suitable for a wide range of fitness levels. Early morning starts are recommended to avoid the crowds and to secure time in the notable cave along the trail. Due to limited parking at the trailhead, hikers are advised to park at the designated nearby school and either start their hike from there or utilize the convenient Sedona Shuttle service.
https://www.fs.usda.gov/recarea/coconino/recarea/?recid=55392

Bell Rock Trailhead

Address: Sedona, AZ 86351

Description: Bell Rock Trailhead offers an unforgettable hiking experience with opportunities to climb to various heights based on your comfort level and tolerance. The trail is a magnet for adventure seekers and nature lovers alike, presenting not only the challenge of the ascent but also breathtaking panoramic views. Early arrival is recommended as parking can fill up quickly, and a pass is required for parking. Whether scaling heights or enjoying a leisurely hike, the trail caters to all with its unique rock formations and vibrant wildlife.
Website: https://www.fs.usda.gov/recarea/coconino/recarea/?recid=55230

Keyhole Cave

Address: Teacup Trail, Sedona, AZ 86336

Description: The Keyhole Cave is a remarkable hiking destination offering spectacular views including Bell Rock, Courthouse, Cathedral Rock, Airport Mesa, and the Village of Oak Creek. However, the trail leading to the cave is not well marked, especially after the split between Teacup Trail/Coffee Pot Rock and Keyhole Cave Trail. It is recommended to keep an eye on the left after the split. The cave itself is impressively large, resembling a two-story building inside, and provides a unique experience that photos or videos cannot fully capture. The hike is generally easy at the start but becomes steeper with looser rocks and vegetation obstacles as you progress. Be advised, parking is limited, with a small lot accommodating only seven cars, and the area tends to fill up quickly on and off season.

Munds Wagon Trail

Address: 167 Schnebly Hill Rd, Sedona, AZ 86336

Description: Munds Wagon Trail is a serene, scenic path perfect for those seeking a tranquil hiking experience. Offering an easy to moderate trail with gentle inclines, it's suitable for most fitness levels. Spanning approximately 4 hours or 8 miles if completing the full loop, hikers can enjoy the lush foliage, stream crossings, and impressive views, especially from the merry-go-round rock. The trail intersects with the jeep road multiple times, adding an interesting dynamic without detracting from the natural beauty. It's an excellent choice for a day hike, offering solitude and stunning landscapes, and is also pet-friendly.

Little Horse Trailhead

Address: AZ-179, Sedona, AZ 86336

Description: Little Horse Trailhead provides a well-maintained path suitable for various activities including biking, hiking, and running. Despite the parking challenges due to its popularity, facilities like public park bathrooms are available for convenience. The trail offers multiple paths for exploration, leading hikers close to Bell Rock with extraordinary views along the way. Despite some rocky sections, the trail's scenic beauty makes it worthwhile, offering stunning landscapes that encapsulate Sedona's iconic red rock vistas.

Broken Arrow Trail

Address: 799 Morgan Rd, Sedona, AZ 86336

Description: The Broken Arrow Trail offers an engaging hiking experience, with clear paths and the unique feature of having a parallel route for off-road vehicles, which intersect with the hiking path at certain points. Hikers can enjoy a vehicle-free experience with occasional mountain bikers. The trail is well-marked with wire cairns and signage at junctions, ensuring an easy-to-follow route amidst stunning scenic views. The trail includes some challenging scrambles but is manageable, extending 3 miles round trip. For a varied experience, hikers can take alternative routes like "High on the Hog" and "Twin Peaks." Note that parking is limited and cannot be anticipated until arrival.

Jim Thompson Trailhead

Address: Jim Thompson Trail, Sedona, AZ 86336

Description: Ideal for early birds looking to avoid the crowds at Soldier Pass, Jim Thompson Trailhead offers 24-hour access and ample parking space. Situated about a mile from the crossroads to Soldier Pass, this trailhead serves as a gateway to several branching trails. Hikers should consult a map beforehand, as the trails are not marked beyond this point. This trailhead is perfect for those looking to explore Sedona's stunning red rock landscapes. Note: The approach road can be rough for low-clearance vehicles, so proceed with caution. The trailhead is equipped with two clean pit toilets, and a Red Rock Pass or America the Beautiful pass is required for parking.

Mescal Trailhead

Address: Mescal Trail, Sedona, AZ 86336

Description: Mescal Trailhead is a favorable starting point for hikers aiming to visit Devil's Bridge with several advantages: more parking availability, shorter distance to the bridge, and no need for a four-wheel-drive vehicle. While the excitement to capture the initial scenic views might be high, conserving energy for the climax at Devil's Bridge is advisable. Note that there could be a waiting time of about 40 minutes for photo opportunities at the bridge, so plan accordingly. The trailhead also features restrooms for convenience. Although the last segment leading to the bridge is rocky, it remains accessible for most hikers. The path from Mescal Trailhead is well-marked, ensuring a hassle-free navigation even for amateur hikers, and offering breathtaking views that reward the effort.

Chapel Trailhead

Address: 780 Chapel Rd, Sedona, AZ 86336
Description: The Chapel Trailhead, adjacent to the iconic Chapel of the Holy Cross, offers a less crowded alternative to Sedona's more popular hiking sites, making it a hidden gem during peak times. This relatively short and accessible trail leads adventurers through stunning red-rock landscapes, culminating in the breathtaking Chicken Point Overlook. The path is well-marked, with frequent vista points that invite hikers to pause and soak in the panoramic views. Connecting to the Little Horse Trail, it provides options for extended exploration and access to renowned scenic spots.

Jordan Road Trailhead

Address: Sedona, AZ 86336
Description: Jordan Road Trailhead serves as a gateway to some of Sedona's most beautiful trails and scenic views. While the access road may be bumpy and require an all-wheel-drive vehicle, the destination offers breathtaking stargazing opportunities and well-maintained facilities, including a clean bathroom and a pass machine. This trailhead is a starting point for various trails, including the one leading to the renowned Seven Sacred Pools. It offers a mix of easy to moderate hiking experiences, with some trails featuring steep inclines and rocky climbs, such as Brins Mesa. Despite these challenges, the trails reward hikers with gorgeous vistas and a serene atmosphere, making it a favorite among Sedona's outdoor enthusiasts.

Raven Caves Trail

Address: Sedona, AZ 86336
Description: Raven Caves Trail offers an accessible yet thrilling adventure for those interested in cave exploration and scenic hikes. This relatively short hike provides an easy route for families and solo travelers alike, leading to peaceful, rocky areas by the river and intriguing caves to explore. Suitable for children and adults, the trail presents moderate difficulty with some steep and tricky sections that require caution. The caves open up to spectacular cliffside views of Sedona's iconic red rocks, making it a worthwhile detour or addition to any hiking day, especially for those coming from nearby attractions like Cathedral Rock.

Schuerman Mountain Trailhead

Address: Sedona, AZ
Description: Schuerman Mountain Trailhead serves as the starting point for two main trails: Scorpion and Pyramid. Scorpion offers a fun yet moderately challenging hike with

enough difficulty to keep the journey engaging without overshadowing the stunning views of Sedona and Red Rock Country. Pyramid Trail, on the other hand, is more rugged and requires greater physical ability but rewards hikers with even more spectacular vistas. Both trails promise an enriching experience for those interested in the natural beauty and wildlife of the area, with the best wildlife viewing opportunities available early in the day.

Parks and Nature

Sedona Wetlands Preserve

Address: 7500 AZ-89A, Sedona, AZ 86336

Description: The Sedona Wetlands Preserve is a serene, environmentally protected area providing a habitat for a variety of wildlife, especially bird species. This unique aquatic ecosystem in the desert environment offers walking paths and viewing platforms for nature observation and photography. It's a peaceful retreat where visitors can experience the natural beauty of Sedona away from the typical tourist spots.

Red Rock State Park

Address: 4050 Red Rock Loop Rd, Sedona, AZ 86336

Description: Red Rock State Park is a 286-acre nature preserve and environmental education center renowned for its stunning red sandstone canyon and verdant riparian habitat. With numerous trails for hiking, opportunities for bird watching, and educational programs, it's an ideal spot for outdoor enthusiasts and families looking to explore the natural splendor of Sedona.

Crescent Moon Picnic Site

Address: 333 Red Rock Crossing Rd, Sedona, AZ 86336

Description: The Crescent Moon Picnic Site, located in the Coconino National Forest, is famous for its splendid views of Cathedral Rock. This picturesque area offers picnic facilities, swimming, and hiking opportunities, making it perfect for a relaxing day out in nature. The site's creekside location provides a cool, shaded environment ideal for summer outings.

Sunset Park

Address: 655 Sunset Dr, Sedona, AZ 86336

Description: Sunset Park is a community-oriented space known for its recreational facilities and scenic beauty. It features a seasonal splash pad, covered playground, sports courts, and open green spaces. Ideal for family outings and social gatherings, the park is a hub of activity where locals and visitors alike can enjoy outdoor fun and festivities.

Amitabha Stupa and Peace Park

Address: 2650 Pueblo Dr, Sedona, AZ 86336

Description: Amitabha Stupa and Peace Park is a spiritual site set amidst Sedona's stunning landscape, offering a tranquil space for meditation and reflection. The park features the Amitabha Stupa, a Buddhist monument symbolizing peace and enlightenment, surrounded by native plants and panoramic views. Visitors of all faiths are welcome to walk the grounds, enjoy the serene atmosphere, and absorb the natural beauty and spiritual energy.

Posse Grounds Park

Address: 525 Posse Ground Rd, Sedona, AZ 86336

Description: Posse Grounds Park is a versatile recreational area in Sedona offering a variety of facilities including sports fields, a skate park, and a community pool. The park caters to all ages with its playgrounds, picnic areas, and walking paths. It is an ideal location for community gatherings, sporting events, and leisurely outdoor activities.

Dry Creek Vista

Address: Chuck Wagon Trail, Sedona, AZ 86336

Description: Dry Creek Vista is a scenic spot known for its breathtaking views of Sedona's famous red rocks and dry creek beds. Easily accessible and offering a peaceful setting, it's a popular place for photography, sightseeing, and contemplation. The vista provides an expansive overview of the area's unique geological features and natural beauty.

Cultural Park Trailhead

Address: 77 Cultural Park Pl #73, Sedona, AZ 86336

Description: The Cultural Park Trailhead serves as the starting point for several hiking trails that explore the rich natural and cultural history of Sedona. The trails offer a blend of scenic views, archaeological sites, and educational opportunities, making it a perfect spot for hikers interested in experiencing the area's historical significance and stunning landscapes.

Sedona Dog Park

Address: 950 Soldiers Pass Rd, Sedona, AZ 86336

Description: Sedona Dog Park is a dedicated space for dogs to play and socialize off-leash. The park features separate areas for large and small dogs, ensuring a safe environment for all. With natural shade, seating for owners, and water stations, it's a welcoming and well-maintained spot for pet owners and their furry friends to enjoy the outdoors.

Garrison Park

Address: 39 Brian Mickelsen Pkwy, Sedona, AZ 86336

Description: Garrison Park is a community space known for its lush greenery and recreational amenities. The park offers sports fields, walking paths, and playgrounds, catering to a range of outdoor activities and family-friendly fun. It's a great place for residents and visitors to unwind, exercise, and enjoy Sedona's natural beauty.

Sunset Park

Address: 655 Sunset Dr, Sedona, AZ 86336

Description: Sunset Park, a vibrant community hub in Sedona, features recreational facilities, picnic areas, and a seasonal splash pad. With its covered playground and expansive open spaces, the park provides a perfect setting for family outings, social gatherings, and outdoor activities, all while offering stunning views of the surrounding red rock landscape.

Accommodation Options
Luxury Resorts

Enchantment Resort
Nestled in Boynton Canyon, this resort offers luxury amidst Sedona's natural beauty, with a renowned spa and exclusive amenities.
Address: 525 Boynton Canyon Rd, Sedona, AZ 86336
Website: https://www.enchantmentresort.com/

L'Auberge de Sedona
A luxury resort set on the banks of Oak Creek, offering elegant accommodations, fine dining, and a tranquil spa.
Address: 301 L'Auberge Ln, Sedona, AZ 86336
Website: https://www.lauberge.com/

Boutique Hotels and Inns

Amara Resort and Spa
A stylish boutique hotel with a modern vibe, centrally located with an infinity pool and spa.
Address: 100 Amara Ln, Sedona, AZ 86336
Website: https://www.amararesort.com/

Sedona Rouge Hotel and Spa
A boutique hotel blending luxury with a touch of the exotic, featuring a full-service spa and gourmet dining.
Address: 2250 W State Rte 89A, Sedona, AZ 86336
Website: https://www.sedonarouge.com/

Bed & Breakfasts

Casa Sedona Inn
A romantic bed and breakfast known for its stunning red rock views and gourmet breakfast.
Address: 55 Hozoni Dr, Sedona, AZ 86336
Website: https://casasedona.com/

Adobe Grand Villas
An intimate B&B offering uniquely themed rooms and personal touches, with a focus on luxury and comfort.
Address: 35 Hozoni Dr, Sedona, AZ 86336
Website: https://adobegrandvillas.com/

Budget-Friendly Options

Arabella Hotel Sedona
A budget-friendly hotel offering comfortable amenities and easy access to Sedona's attractions.
Address: 725 AZ-179, Sedona, AZ 86336
Website: https://www.arabellahotelsedona.com/

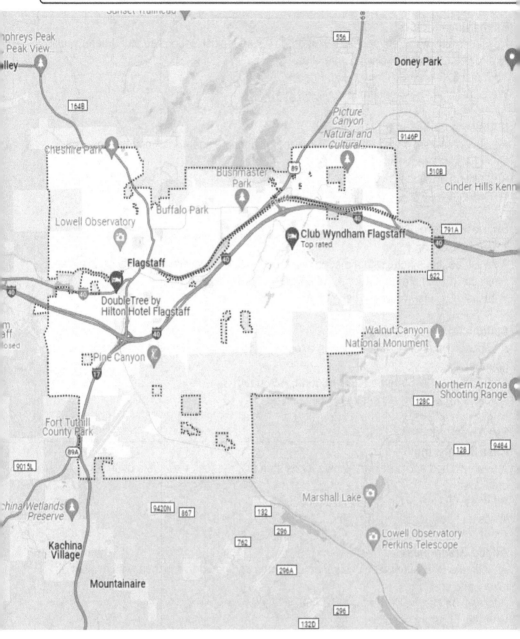

Flagstaff, Arizona, beautifully nestled in the mountains of Northern Arizona, serves as a quintessential gateway to the Grand Canyon and a haven for outdoor enthusiasts. This charming city, with its rich history, scientific significance, and access to stunning natural landscapes, offers a unique blend of experiences for its visitors.

The list below includes a wide range of tourist attractions located in Flagstaff and the surrounding vicinity.

Museums

Museum of Northern Arizona

Address: 3101 N Fort Valley Rd, Flagstaff, AZ 86001
Hours: 10 AM–5 PM daily
Description: The Museum of Northern Arizona is a tastefully curated space that delves into a diverse range of subjects, from geographic to rich history of Native American culture. Despite its unassuming exterior, the museum surprises visitors with its expansive interior, boasting numerous exhibit rooms that offer an enriching experience. Plan to spend at least three hours to fully appreciate the depth of its offerings.
While past attractions like the STAR WARS EXHIBIT and R2D2 are no longer available, the museum continues to captivate with its array of interesting pieces and exhibits. However, visitors should be aware that the gift shop, while housing beautiful and unique items, tends to be pricey. It lacks an affordable children's section, which may disappoint younger visitors hoping for a memento. Despite this drawback, the museum itself is well worth the visit, offering a blend of education and entertainment for all ages. Additionally, there's a random ant play area that younger children may enjoy.
Website: https://musnaz.org/

Riordan Mansion State Historic Park

Address: 409 W Riordan Rd, Flagstaff, AZ 86001
Hours: 9:30 AM–5 PM daily
Description: Riordan Mansion State Historic Park offers visitors a glimpse into the rich history of Northern Arizona, specifically highlighting the legacy of the Riordan family in the milling and forestry industry. The park features a beautifully maintained mansion surrounded by picturesque landscapes.
Visitors have the option of a self-guided tour for $2 or a guided tour for $12, which allows access inside the mansion. Guided tours are scheduled hourly and accommodate a limited number of guests, ensuring a personalized experience. The rangers at the mansion are praised for their friendliness and extensive knowledge, enhancing the visit. Exploring the mansion provides insight into the Riordans' contributions to art awareness and fair treatment of workers, adding depth to their legacy. The immaculate condition of the home further emphasizes its significance in preserving the history of Northern Arizona. Overall, Riordan Mansion State Historic Park is a must-see for anyone interested in the region's history and the impact of influential families like the Riordans.
Website: https://azstateparks.com/riordan-mansion/

Elden Pueblo Archaeological Site

Address: US-89, Flagstaff, AZ 86004
Website: http://www.fs.usda.gov/recarea/coconino/recarea/?recid=55092
Description: The Elden Pueblo Archaeological Site provides a fascinating insight into early native life in Northern Arizona. This active archaeological site allows visitors to explore the remnants of ancient civilizations, with ongoing discoveries still being made. While the site offers an easy walk, visitors may find it more serene to visit in the evening when traffic noise from the nearby highway is reduced. Be sure to scan the QR code at the entrance to learn more about the site's history and significance.

Pioneer Museum–Arizona Historical Society

Status: Temporarily closed due to insufficient staff to operate the entire museum
Address: 2340 N Fort Valley Rd, Flagstaff, AZ 86001
Website: https://arizonahistoricalsociety.org/museum/pioneer-museum/
Description: The Pioneer Museum, part of the Arizona Historical Society, is a captivating destination for history enthusiasts and those curious about Arizona's past. While temporarily closed, it typically offers a wealth of exhibits housed in various buildings, including the main house (formerly a hospital), a barn, a train, and several other structures. Visitors praise the museum for its comprehensive exploration of Arizona's history, making it a highly recommended stop for travelers eager to delve into the region's rich heritage.

The Artists' Gallery

Address: 17 N San Francisco St, Flagstaff, AZ 86001
Hours: Friday to Wednesday: 10 AM–6 PM, Sunday: 11 AM–4 PM
Website: https://theflagstaffartistsgallery.com/
Description: The Artists' Gallery showcases an impressive collection of local art, featuring works by talented Flagstaff artists. Visitors can explore a wide variety of art mediums, including jewelry, paintings, scarves, pottery, and more. The gallery's staff is praised for their friendliness, knowledge, and helpfulness, ensuring a pleasant and enjoyable shopping experience. With its deceptively large space, the gallery offers an abundance of unique pieces, making it a perfect destination for finding gifts or adding to your art collection.

Tynkertopia, Inc.

Address: 3330 E Elder Dr, Flagstaff, AZ 86004
Hours: Friday: 1:30–6 PM, Saturday: 10 AM–4 PM, Sunday & Monday: Closed
Tuesday to Thursday: 1–6 PM
Website: https://www.tynkertopia.org/
Description: Tynkertopia, Inc. offers an engaging and creative space for children of all ages to explore, learn, and play. With a variety of activities and materials available, including art supplies, building materials, and robotics, children can immerse themselves in hands-on projects and experiments. Visitors commend the cleanliness of the facility and the range of activities suitable for toddlers and older kids alike.
Many families find themselves returning to Tynkertopia, Inc. regularly, as the space provides endless opportunities for fun and learning. Whether it's crafting cards, building tracks, programming robots, or simply tinkering with supplies, children are sure to have a fantastic time. The facility also hosts after-hours birthday parties, offering a hassle-free and enjoyable experience for both kids and adults. Overall, Tynkertopia, Inc. is highly recommended for families seeking a dynamic and enriching play environment.

Historical Sites and Monuments

Walnut Canyon National Monument

Admission: $25.00

Address: Official site: https://www.nps.gov/waca/index.htm

Hours: Friday to Thursday: 9 AM–4:30 PM

Description: Walnut Canyon National Monument offers visitors a captivating journey through history amidst stunning natural scenery. The visitor experience includes a comprehensive film providing insights into the area's rich history, complemented by helpful rangers who are available to answer questions and provide guidance.

The monument features over 900 stairs for adventurous hikers, offering an immersive exploration of the canyon's historical dwellings. The dwellings, built within the canyon where water has undercut the rocks, create a unique and awe-inspiring sight. The visitor center, though small, provides valuable information, including a 20-minute film that sets the stage for the exploration ahead.

Two trails originate from the visitor center: the Island Trail, a 1-mile trek that descends into the canyon, providing up-close views of the dwellings and informative interpretive signs about the history, geology, and plant life; and a shorter trail along the rim for those who prefer to admire the scenery from above.

Lowell Observatory

Address: 1400 W Mars Hill Rd, Flagstaff, AZ 86001

Hours: Friday to Sunday, Wednesday, Thursday: 12–10 PM, Monday & Tuesday: Closed

Website: https://lowell.edu/welcomeback

Admission: $29.00

Description: Lowell Observatory is a must-visit destination in Flagstaff, offering an immersive exploration of the cosmos and celestial wonders. The observatory is renowned for its pivotal role in the discovery of Pluto and houses several fascinating exhibits and facilities, including:

- Giovale Open Deck Observatory (GODO)
- Clark Telescope
- Steele Visitor Center
- Putnam Collection Center
- Lowell Titan Monitor (TiMo) Telescope
- Astronomy Discovery Center
- Rotunda Museum

Visitors commend the observatory for its captivating exhibits, informative tours, and friendly, knowledgeable staff. The tours provide valuable insights into the observatory's history and scientific achievements without overwhelming visitors. Guests are encouraged to arrive early to take advantage of the tours and then return in the evening for telescope viewing of the stars and planets. Admission tickets are valid all day, allowing visitors to leave and return as they please.

Situated at a high elevation, Lowell Observatory offers a stunning view of the night sky, making it an ideal location for stargazing. However, visitors should be prepared for cooler temperatures, especially in the evenings. Packing warm layers of clothing ensures a comfortable and enjoyable experience under the clear night skies.

Flagstaff Area National Monuments

Address: 6400 US-89, Flagstaff, AZ 86004
Hours:
Friday, Monday to Thursday: 8:30 AM–4:30 PM
Saturday & Sunday: Closed
Website: https://www.nps.gov/waca/learn/management/flag_parks.htm
Description: The Flagstaff Area National Monuments offer a wealth of educational and scenic experiences for visitors. Information about Walnut Canyon or Wupatki/Sunset Crater is available at the parks. These monuments serve as excellent destinations for learning and stimulating the mind, providing opportunities to explore the natural and cultural wonders of the region.

Sunset Crater Volcano National Monument

Address: Sunset Crater Volcano is just twelve miles north of Flagstaff, Arizona on U.S. 89.
Description: Sunset Crater Volcano National Monument is home to an 8,042-ft. extinct cinder cone, offering visitors a chance to marvel at ancient lava flows. The monument features a 1-mile loop trail at the base of the crater for exploration. Admission to the monument is $25, providing access to the remarkable geological formations and scenic vistas.

Visitors describe the experience as simply awesome, with opportunities to observe the lava flows and enjoy scenic walkways around the crater. The area offers picturesque viewpoints, allowing visitors to capture stunning images of Sunset Crater and the surrounding snow-capped mountains. For science enthusiasts intrigued by volcanoes, Sunset Crater Volcano National Monument is a must-visit destination, offering insights into the fascinating world of volcanic activity and igneous rock formations.

Gold King Mine & Ghost Town

Address: Perkinsville Rd, Jerome, AZ 86331
Hours: Friday to Wednesday: 9 AM–5 PM | Thursday: Closed
Website: http://www.goldkingmineghosttown.com/
Description: Gold King Mine & Ghost Town offers a unique and quirky stop for visitors, featuring dilapidated buildings, an old mine, and a vast collection of vintage automobiles and trucks. Situated in Jerome, Arizona, this funky attraction provides a glimpse into the region's mining history and boasts a charming array of farm animals, including chickens, a potbelly pig, and three goats.

Visitors praise the friendly and informative staff who enhance the experience with their knowledge and hospitality. The attraction offers a variety of activities, including gem sifting, gold panning, geode cracking, and animal feeding, providing fun and entertainment for visitors of all ages. For an immersive experience, guests can opt for the $38 special package, which includes a range of interactive activities and hands-on experiences.

While exploring Gold King Mine & Ghost Town, visitors can immerse themselves in the ambiance of a bygone era, surrounded by vintage vehicles and mining equipment of various sizes. The drive up the mountain to reach the town of Jerome adds to the adventure, offering picturesque views along the way.

Parks and Outdoor Activities

Buffalo Park

Address: 2400 N Gemini Rd, Flagstaff, AZ 86004
Hours: Friday to Thursday: 5 AM–10 PM
Website: https://www.flagstaff.az.gov/1923/City-Parks-Ramadas
Description: Buffalo Park offers a picturesque outdoor experience in Flagstaff, Arizona, featuring beautiful hiking trails suitable for beginners and families. The park boasts flat loops with stunning views, making it an ideal destination for those seeking a leisurely outdoor adventure. Visitors can enjoy the park's dog-friendly atmosphere while taking in the fantastic scenery.

This local gem is renowned for its easy-to-navigate trails, including a popular 2-mile loop that is perfect for walking, running, and biking. The park is also part of the Arizona Trail, providing additional opportunities for exploration and adventure. With sweeping views of the San Francisco Peaks, Buffalo Park offers a convenient escape to nature for residents and visitors alike.

Picture Canyon Natural and Cultural Preserve

Address: 3920 N El Paso Flagstaff Rd, Flagstaff, AZ 86004
Description: Picture Canyon Natural and Cultural Preserve is a 478-acre nature preserve located in Flagstaff, Arizona, offering a blend of outdoor recreation and cultural heritage. The preserve features hiking, biking, and horseback riding trails, providing visitors with a chance to explore the area's diverse landscapes and wildlife.

Visitors to Picture Canyon can enjoy beautiful trails that cater to various skill levels, with options ranging from mild to moderate inclines. The trail system is well-maintained and fairly well-signed, ensuring a pleasant hiking experience. One of the highlights of the preserve is the opportunity to view petroglyphs left behind by the Northern Sinagua people, offering a fascinating glimpse into the region's Native American heritage.

While exploring the trails, visitors can immerse themselves in the preserve's natural beauty, which includes a waterfall and dense trees providing ample shade. However, it's worth noting that the preserve is located near a wastewater plant, and there may be a slight odor near the beginning of the hike.

Fort Tuthill County Park

Address: 2446 Ft Tuthill Lp, Flagstaff, AZ 86005
Hours: Friday, Monday to Thursday: 8 AM–5 PM, Saturday, Sunday: Closed
Description: Fort Tuthill County Park offers a sprawling recreational area nestled in the scenic landscape of Flagstaff, Arizona. This diverse park features a range of amenities and activities for visitors of all ages, making it an ideal destination for outdoor enthusiasts and families alike.

The park encompasses archery and equestrian facilities, along with expansive trails that wind through the picturesque surroundings. Visitors can enjoy hiking, running, or biking on the well-marked trails, which offer a combination of smooth pathways and challenging terrain. The Soldiers Loop trail is a popular choice for runners seeking a scenic workout. Additionally, Fort Tuthill County Park is home to various adventure courses and outdoor attractions, including the Flagstaff Extreme Adventure Course and Flagstaff Snow Park.

The park's Pepsi Amphitheater hosts a variety of events, providing entertainment and cultural enrichment for visitors.

For those seeking overnight accommodations, the park offers camping options at the Fort Tuthill County Campground, featuring forest tent and RV sites. The campground provides a convenient base for exploring the park's numerous amenities and nearby attractions.

Foxglenn Park

Address: 4200 E Butler Ave, Flagstaff, AZ 86004
Hours: Friday to Thursday: 6 AM–9 PM
Website: flagstaffarizona.org/flagstaff_locations/foxglenn-park

Foxglenn Park is a beloved recreational destination nestled in the heart of Flagstaff, Arizona. This expansive park offers a wide range of amenities and activities, making it a favorite spot for locals and visitors alike.

The park boasts ample space for outdoor play and relaxation, with sprawling grassy areas perfect for picnics, sports, and leisurely strolls. Families can enjoy the playground, which features a variety of equipment designed for children of all ages. The mommy-daughter double swing is a popular attraction, providing a fun bonding experience for parents and kids.

Sports enthusiasts will appreciate the basketball court and skate park, offering opportunities for active recreation and skill-building. The park's well-maintained trails provide a scenic backdrop for walking, jogging, or biking, with opportunities to spot local wildlife along the way. While enjoying the park, be sure to bring along plenty of water, as the water fountain may not be operational. However, clean restrooms are available near the skate park, ensuring convenience for visitors.

Thorpe Park

Address: 191 N Thorpe Rd, Flagstaff, AZ 86001
Hours: Friday to Thursday: 5 AM–12 AM

Thorpe Park offers a tranquil retreat amidst the bustling city of Flagstaff, Arizona. Nestled within a verdant landscape, this park provides a serene setting for relaxation, recreation, and outdoor enjoyment.

Visitors to Thorpe Park are greeted by the beauty of nature, with majestic trees, lush grass, and spacious areas for picnics and gatherings.

Picnic tables and grills are strategically placed throughout the park, providing convenient spots for outdoor dining and barbecues. The generous spacing between picnic areas ensures privacy and comfort for park visitors.

Rogers Lake County Natural Area

Address: 10 miles southwest of Flagstaff on Woody Mountain Road / Forest Road 231, Flagstaff, AZ 86001
Hours: Friday to Thursday: 6 AM–10 PM
Website: www.oconino.az.gov/parks/rogerslake

This expansive natural area offers a picturesque setting for hiking, strolling, and immersing oneself in the beauty of Northern Arizona's landscape.

Navigating the well-maintained trails of Rogers Lake County Natural Area, visitors are treated to breathtaking views of the surrounding wilderness. The area's diverse ecosystems provide habitat for a variety of flora and fauna, making it a haven for nature lovers and wildlife enthusiasts alike.

One of the highlights of Rogers Lake County Natural Area is the opportunity for hiking adventures. Families can embark on leisurely strolls or more challenging hikes, exploring the area's rugged terrain and discovering hidden gems along the way. For those seeking a longer excursion, a five-mile hike to a fire watch tower offers panoramic vistas of the surrounding landscape, including views of the Sports Dome at Northern Arizona University.

Thorpe Park Sports & Recreation Complex

Address: 191 N Thorpe Rd, Flagstaff, AZ 86001
Hours: Friday to Wednesday: 5 AM–10 PM, Thursday: 5 AM–12 AM
Website: flagstaff.az.gov/1923/City-Parks-Ramadas

Thorpe Park Sports & Recreation Complex is a versatile destination offering a range of activities and amenities for residents and visitors alike. Located in the heart of Flagstaff, Arizona, this expansive complex provides opportunities for outdoor recreation, sports, and leisurely pursuits.

Within the complex, visitors will find various attractions and facilities, including:

1. **Thorpe Park:** A scenic park area surrounded by lush greenery and offering ample space for picnics, leisurely walks, and outdoor gatherings.
2. **Frances Short Pond:** A tranquil pond where visitors can enjoy fishing, birdwatching, or simply relaxing by the water's edge.
3. **Church for the Nations Flagstaff:** A place of worship and community gathering, providing spiritual enrichment and fellowship opportunities.
4. **Thorpe Park Ball Fields:** Well-maintained ball fields ideal for sports enthusiasts to engage in recreational activities such as baseball, softball, or soccer.
5. **Original Flagstaff Replica:** A historical landmark commemorating the city's heritage and serving as a reminder of its rich history and cultural significance.
6. **Dog Park:** A dedicated space for canine companions to exercise, socialize, and play under the supervision of their owners. The dog park features various obstacles and amenities for both dogs and their owners to enjoy.

Griffith Spring Trailhead

Trail Description: Griffith Spring Trailhead offers a pleasant and accessible hiking experience, suitable for individuals of all skill levels. The mile-long loop trail provides scenic views and opportunities for outdoor recreation.
Amenities: Picnic tables are available for visitors to enjoy outdoor meals or snacks. However, please note that the bathroom facilities are currently closed.
Regulations: Camping and campfires are not permitted in the area.
Operating Hours: Friday to Thursday: 6 AM–10 PM

Sycamore Falls

Address: Williams, AZ 86046
Description: Sycamore Falls is a hidden gem, offering breathtaking views even during its dry winter state. Despite the minimal hike required to reach it, the destination provides an incredibly peaceful ambiance and stunning scenery, perfect for nature lovers and those

seeking a break from the hustle and bustle of urban life. While the falls might not always be brimming with water, the surrounding landscapes remain impressively beautiful, ensuring a worthwhile visit.

Campbell Mesa Loop Trails

Address: Forest Service Rd 790, Flagstaff, AZ 86004
Description: Campbell Mesa Loop Trails offer a wonderfully peaceful escape ideal for less experienced hikers or those simply looking to enjoy a serene walk in nature. The trails are relatively flat, making them perfect for a casual stroll or a dog walk. Visitors should be mindful of the occasional cyclist. Despite the lack of public restrooms, the area is well-loved for its accessibility, ample parking, and breathtaking views of Mt Elden and other peaks in the San Francisco range.

Grand Canyon Deer Farm LLC

Address: 6769 Deer Farm Rd, Williams, AZ 86046
Description: Grand Canyon Deer Farm LLC is an enchanting family-friendly attraction where visitors, especially children, can interact with and feed friendly deer and other animals. The farm offers a unique experience where the deer roam freely and interact with guests. The entrance fee includes feed for the animals, ensuring an engaging visit for all ages. It's a great place for animal lovers and families looking for a fun day outing, with plenty of opportunities for close-up encounters with various gentle creatures.
Opening Hours: Sunday – Monday 10AM – 5PM
Website: http://www.deerfarm.com/

Fatman's Loop Trail

Address: 5098 US-89, Flagstaff, AZ 86004
Description: Fatman's Loop Trail is a popular hiking destination offering scenic views and unique geological formations. The trail is known for its volcanic rock landscapes and moderate difficulty, making it suitable for hikers of various skill levels. It's an ideal spot for those looking to experience the natural beauty of the Flagstaff area without committing to an overly strenuous hike.
Opening Hours: Open daily, closes at 10 PM.

Mt Elden Lookout Trail

Address: 4870, 5098 US-89, Flagstaff, AZ 86004
Description: Mt Elden Lookout Trail is a challenging hike that rewards adventurers with breathtaking panoramic views from the summit. The trail is well-known for its significant elevation gain, making it ideal for experienced hikers seeking a rigorous outdoor activity. The top of the trail provides spectacular views of Flagstaff and the surrounding areas.
Opening Hours: Open daily, closes at 10 PM.

Pumphouse Wash Trailhead

Address: Pumphouse Wash can be accessed from areas along Highway 89A south of Flagstaff. Please check local resources for the exact trailhead location.
Description: Pumphouse Wash Trailhead marks the beginning of a picturesque trail through a canyon filled with diverse vegetation and streambeds. It's favored for its serene

environment and the opportunity to experience the unique riparian ecosystems of northern Arizona.

Sedona Bike Skills Park

Address: 525 Posse Ground Rd, Sedona, AZ 86336

Description: The Sedona Bike Skills Park is designed for cyclists of all ages and skill levels to practice and enhance their mountain biking skills. The park features various trails, jumps, and pump tracks, catering to everyone from beginners to advanced riders seeking to improve their techniques and have fun.

Opening Hours: Closes 9 PM.

Humphreys Peak Trail

Address: Humphreys Summit Trail, Flagstaff, AZ 86001

Description: Humphreys Peak Trail is the route to the highest point in Arizona, offering challenging hikes with significant elevation gain. The trail is known for its breathtaking views, alpine tundra, and rigorous terrain. It's a must-do for seasoned hikers seeking to conquer Arizona's highest summit and experience the state from its most awe-inspiring vantage point.

Opening Hours: Open 24 hours.

Recreational and Adventure Sites

Levitate Adventure Park

Address: 4601 E Marketplace Dr, 4601 E Railhead Ave, Flagstaff, AZ 86004

Description: Levitate Adventure Park is an exceptional family-friendly destination in Flagstaff, designed with attention to every detail to ensure a fun-filled experience for both children and adults. The park boasts spacious areas for jumping, a dedicated bounce house that children adore, and special events like toddler time. Beyond the trampolines, the venue offers delicious pizza and ice cream, making it an ideal spot for family outings and fun.

Opening Hours: Sunday: 9 AM – 8 PM, Monday - Thursday: 10 AM – 8 PM, Friday: 10 AM – 10 PM, Saturday: 9 AM – 10 PM

Website: http://www.levitate.fun

Arizona Snowbowl

Address: 9300 N Snow Bowl Rd, Flagstaff, AZ 86001

Description: Arizona Snowbowl stands out as a breathtaking outdoor haven perfect for those who love nature and adventure. The Aspen Trail Loop offers scenic hiking experiences with ample parking and helpful signage. Visitors can also enjoy the gondola ride to the summit, where stunning views and cool temperatures await. Despite being a bit chilly at 11,500 feet, the top of the mountain offers unparalleled scenic beauty and wildlife spotting opportunities. The base area offers a warm atmosphere with live music and hot cocoa, making for a perfect relaxation spot after a day of activities. While dining options are available, bringing your own food might be a better choice due to potential long waits and limited menu items during peak times.

Opening Hours: Open daily from 9 AM to 4 PM, Arizona Snowbowl welcomes visitors throughout the week, offering a variety of outdoor activities from serene hikes to exhilarating gondola rides.
Website: http://www.snowbowl.ski/

Canyon Ministries – Grand Canyon Christian Tours & Adventures

Address: 2727 W Rte 66, Flagstaff, AZ 86001
Description: Canyon Ministries offers unique Christian-based tours of the Grand Canyon, providing insights into the natural wonders from a biblical perspective. These tours are designed to explore the geological and spiritual significance of the Grand Canyon, making it a memorable experience for believers and curious visitors alike.
Website: https://www.canyonministries.org/

Visitor Centers and Informational Sites

Flagstaff Visitor Center

1 E Rte 66, Flagstaff, AZ 86001
Description: The Flagstaff Visitor Center is a prime starting point for tourists and visitors in Flagstaff, conveniently located within the Amtrak station. Offering an array of cool knickknacks, local artist merchandise like stickers and shirts, and a charming toy train display, it's the perfect introduction to the area. Just steps away from the bustling downtown, it provides easy access to thrift stores, outdoor outfitters, bars, and restaurants. The center is ideal for pedestrians and cyclists alike, making it an excellent spot for launching your Flagstaff adventure. Additionally, for Pokémon GO enthusiasts, the downtown area around the center is rich with gyms and PokéStops, adding an extra layer of fun to the visit.
Opening Hours:
- Open from 8 AM to 5 PM on Fridays, Saturdays, Mondays, Tuesdays, Wednesdays, and Thursdays.
- Sunday hours are slightly shorter, from 9 AM to 4 PM.
Website: Flagstaff Visitor Center

Meteor Crater Visitor Center

Meteor Crater Rd, Winslow, AZ 86047
Description: Meteor Crater Visitor Center is a unique and educational destination off Route 66, providing visitors with a comprehensive self-guided tour of this remarkable natural landmark. With Dawn's welcoming presence at the front desk and knowledgeable tour guides, visitors gain valuable insights into the history and science of the meteor strike. The center is well-equipped with comfortable theater seating and interactive learning stations, ensuring an educational experience for all ages. Clean facilities are available, and the site offers discounts for military and AAA members. Note: the entrance fee is $29. Be prepared for windy and chilly conditions on the observation decks by dressing appropriately.
Opening Hours:
- Open daily from 8 AM to 5 PM.
Website: http://meteorcrater.com/

Accommodation Options
Little America Hotel Flagstaff
Nestled within a 500-acre pine forest, this hotel offers luxurious amenities, fine dining, and a tranquil setting. **Address:** 2515 E Butler Ave, Flagstaff, AZ 86004

Twin Arrows Navajo Casino Resort
A luxury resort with modern amenities, casino entertainment, dining options, and well-appointed rooms.
Address: 22181 Resort Blvd, Flagstaff, AZ 86004 | Website: https://www.twinarrows.com/

Boutique Hotels and Inns
Hotel Monte Vista
A historic and iconic hotel in downtown Flagstaff, known for its unique charm and storied past. **Address:** 100 N San Francisco St, Flagstaff, AZ 86001
Website: https://www.hotelmontevista.com/

Weatherford Hotel
Another historic hotel offering a glimpse into Flagstaff's past, with Victorian-era decor and a cozy atmosphere.
Address: 23 N Leroux St, Flagstaff, AZ 86001 | Website: https://weatherfordhotel.com/

Mid-Range Hotels
Drury Inn & Suites Flagstaff
Offers comfortable accommodations with free breakfast and evening snacks, located near Northern Arizona University. **Address:** 300 S Milton Rd, Flagstaff, AZ 86001

Hilton Garden Inn Flagstaff
A reliable choice for comfortable lodging with modern amenities and a convenient location.
Address: 350 W Forest Meadows St, Flagstaff, AZ 86001

Budget-Friendly Options
GreenTree Inn Flagstaff
A budget-friendly hotel offering essential amenities and comfort.
Address: 2755 S Woodlands Village Blvd, Flagstaff, AZ 86001
Website: https://www.greentreeinn.com/

Starlight Pines Bed and Breakfast
A Victorian-style B&B offering a quaint and peaceful setting with beautiful rooms.
Address: 3380 E Lockett Rd, Flagstaff, AZ 86004 | Website: https://starlightpinesbb.com/

Bed and Breakfasts
England House Bed and Breakfast
A charming B&B in a historic building, offering a cozy stay with personalized service.
Address: 614 W Santa Fe Ave, Flagstaff, AZ 86001 | www.englandhousebandb.com/

Antelope Canyon

Located in the American Southwest, beyond the majestic expanses of the Grand Canyon, lies another natural marvel that captivates visitors with its ethereal beauty – Antelope Canyon. This slot canyon, part of the Navajo Nation in Northern Arizona, is celebrated for its extraordinary wave-like structures and the mesmerizing play of light within its narrow corridors.

Antelope Canyon's Unique Formation

Antelope Canyon is a slot canyon, which means it is significantly deeper than it is wide. Formed by the erosion of Navajo sandstone, primarily due to flash flooding and other sub-aerial processes, the canyon's corridors are smooth and flowing in appearance, creating a wave-like effect.

The canyon is divided into two separate sections, commonly referred to as "The Upper Antelope Canyon" or "The Crack" and "The Lower Antelope Canyon" or "The Corkscrew." Each section offers a distinctly different experience due to their unique geology.

The Play of Light

One of the most striking features of Antelope Canyon is the way sunlight filters down through the narrow openings at the top, creating beams of light that illuminate the sandy floor below. This natural interplay of light and shadow highlights the red-orange hues of the canyon walls, creating a surreal and almost otherworldly experience.

The best time to witness these light beams is around midday, particularly in the summer months, when the sun is at its highest point and the light can penetrate deep into the canyon.

Visiting Antelope Canyon

Access to Antelope Canyon is regulated and managed by the Navajo Nation, and all visits must be part of a guided tour. These tours are led by knowledgeable guides who can provide insights into the canyon's geology, history, and cultural significance.

Location: Tse'Bii'Ndzisgaii – Monument Valley
Address: Monument Valley, UT 84536
GPS Coordinates: N 37.00414 W 110.09889
Elevation: 5,564 feet above sea level
Size: 91,696 acres (spans across Utah & Arizona)
Overview: Monument Valley Navajo Tribal Park stands as a symbol of the majestic and the most photographed landscapes on Earth. Within its boundaries, sandstone towers soar between 400 to 1,000 feet into the sky, set against a backdrop of the vast, colorful desert expanse. This landscape overwhelms with its immense beauty, offering a blend of fragile rock pinnacles, mesas, buttes, and the ever-shifting sands, presenting a palette of nature's finest colors.
Visiting Hours:
Park/Administration Office:
Winter: 8:00 am to 5:00 pm, Monday-Friday
Summer: Extended hours apply for the scenic drive and tour booth
Scenic Drive:
Winter: 8:00 am to 5:00 pm, Monday – Sunday (Last Entry at 2:30 pm)
Summer: 7:00 am to 7:00 pm, Monday – Sunday (Last Entry: 4:30 pm)
Entry Fee: $8 per person, per day. Fees for additional persons and special activities may apply.
Experiences:
17-Mile Loop Drive: A must-do for every visitor, this loop drive offers spectacular views of the valley's iconic formations. Note that motorcycles and RVs are prohibited due to the challenging terrain, including deep sand dunes and rough patches, especially during the monsoon season.

Hiking: The Wildcat Trail offers a 1.5-mile hike, showcasing the valley from the ground level. Hikers need to sign in/out at the Visitor Center and obtain a Backcountry Permit for extended explorations.

Cultural Encounters: Engage with local vendors along the loop road for handcrafted jewelry and artifacts, providing a tangible connection to Navajo artistry and traditions.

Traveler's Note:
Visitors should prepare for varied conditions, including long wait times during peak season (May to September) and unpredictable weather. Appropriate attire, including hats, t-shirts, long sleeves, and tennis shoes, is recommended for comfort and protection. Staying hydrated is crucial in the desert climate to prevent heat exhaustion and dehydration.

Special Permissions:
For photography, filming, weddings, and other land usages, a Special Use Permit is required. Please visit the Visitor Center for details.

Safety Advisory:
The Navajo Parks and Recreation Department advises caution on the loop drive, as it is not liable for any vehicle damage on Navajo Tribal Park land. Always stay on designated routes and respect the natural and cultural integrity of this iconic landscape.

Closure Information:
The park observes major holiday closures in line with the Navajo Nation calendar, including Thanksgiving Day, Christmas Day, and New Year's Day.

For More Information:
To plan your visit or purchase entry tickets, please refer to the official Monument Valley website. This site provides detailed information on hours, fees, and conditions to ensure a memorable and respectful visit to this revered Navajo Nation landmark.

Website: https://navajonationparks.org/tribal-parks/monument-valley/

Petrified Forest National Park

Description: Petrified Forest National Park, renowned for its vast collection of petrified wood, presents a unique blend of natural wonders and historical narratives. Despite the three-hour drive from Phoenix, the journey to the park is a gateway to exploring the vibrantly colored landscapes of the Painted Desert and a diverse array of geological formations. The park offers an immersive experience into the prehistoric past, showcasing the transformation of organic material into stone through the petrified wood scattered throughout. The diverse terrain reveals a palette of colors that change with the weather, especially pronounced after rain, enhancing the dramatic visual impact.

Visitors can embark on a journey through the park, facilitated by a $25 vehicle pass valid for seven days, ensuring ample time to explore each significant site and trail. The park is divided into various sectors, each narrating a distinct aspect of its ancient and ecological history, complemented by detailed placards. Noteworthy for its visitor-friendly amenities, the park accommodates pets and provides accessibility for all, featuring paved paths and ample parking. An important advisory for visitors: adhere to safety guidelines, particularly the caution against roaming after 5:30 PM due to wildlife activity, notably coyotes. This ensures a safe and enjoyable experience as you explore the park's wonders.

Entry Fee: $25.00 per vehicle (pass valid for 7 days)
Opening Hours: Daily 8 AM – 6 PM
Website: https://www.nps.gov/pefo/index.htm
Known for its large deposits of petrified wood, along with colorful badlands, and ancient petroglyphs.

Vermilion Cliffs National Monument

Vermilion Cliffs National Monument, a sprawling 280,000-acre landscape, stands as a testament to the raw and untamed beauty of geology. This monument, rich in diverse landscapes like the Paria Plateau, Vermilion Cliffs, Coyote Buttes, and Paria Canyon, borders the Kaibab National Forest and Glen Canyon National Recreation Area. It boasts elevations from 3,100 to 7,100 feet and is a sanctuary for the endangered California condor, with annual releases from a captive breeding program.

Road Access:
From Flagstaff: Travel north on U.S. Highway 89, connecting to U.S. Highway 89A at the Bitter Springs turnoff.
From Kanab, Utah: East on U.S. 89 or south on U.S. 89A through Fredonia and Jacob Lake.
Navigation:
Within its boundaries, the monument challenges visitors with its absence of paved roads. House Rock Valley Road (BLM 1065) offers a maintained dirt road option, though it can become impassable when wet. For the rest, a high-clearance, four-wheel-drive vehicle is essential due to deep sand conditions.
Activities:
The monument is a haven for outdoor enthusiasts, offering:
- Scenic views of immense cliffs and deep canyons.
- Wilderness backpacking in Paria Canyon (3-5 days, permits required).
- The mesmerizing cross-bedded sandstone of Coyote Buttes.
- Wildlife viewing, including the opportunity to see California condors.
Camping:
Developed Campgrounds: Stateline and White House, located outside the monument.
Dispersed Camping: Permitted in designated areas outside the wilderness zone.
Permits:
Essential for Coyote Buttes North (The Wave), Coyote Buttes South, and overnight stays in Paria Canyon.
Facilities:
No visitor centers are available within the monument. However, Arizona Strip visitor maps and further information can be obtained online or at:
- Paria Contact Station https://www.blm.gov/visit/paria-contact-station
- BLM Kanab Visitor Center https://www.blm.gov/visit/kanab-visitor-center
Safety Tips:
Preparation is key. Travelers should be ready for:
- Rugged and unmarked terrain
- Potential encounters with venomous wildlife
- Extreme weather conditions, including heat, cold, and flash floods
- Essential supplies: A full-size spare tire, ample water, food, and gasoline

Other attractions within the park
The Wave: A striking red sandstone formation known for its picturesque landscapes.
White Pocket: Offers breathtaking scenery, characterized by its unique geological formations.
Condor Viewing Site: A prime location for witnessing the majestic California condors in their natural habitat.
Dominguez Escalante Expedition Monument: A historical site offering insights into the significant expedition by Dominguez and Escalante.
The Second Wave: Another beautiful rock formation, though not as famed as The Wave, offering scenic views.
Melody Arch: A picturesque arch that's a highlight for hikers in the area.

*Description: **The Wave***

The Alcove: Known for its spectacular natural beauty, making it a worthwhile destination for hikers.

Cottonwood Teepees Trailhead: The starting point for an amazing experience at Coyote Buttes South, featuring unique rock formations.

The Big Mac: A challenging but rewarding part of The Wave Trail, requiring experience and thorough preparation.

Vermilion Cliffs National Monument Bulletin Board: Provides visitors with information and updates about the park.

Vermilion Cliffs Condor Release Viewing Area: A vista point for observing California condors released into the wild.

North Teepees: A scenic spot featuring unique geological structures that resemble teepees.

The Southern Wave: Offers unmarked trails leading to stunning rock formations; preparation is key.

Mini Wave: Known for its strenuous hike leading to rewarding views, reminiscent of the larger Wave formation.

Sun Valley Mine Trailhead: An easy hike that leads to colorful area ruins, showcasing the area's mining history.

Dinosaur Tracks: A scenic spot where visitors can view preserved dinosaur tracks.

Top Rock Arch: Provides an elevated view of the surrounding area from atop a rock arch.

White Pocket Trailhead: The starting point for hikes in the White Pocket area, known for its surreal landscapes.

Sand Cove: A cool and unreal hiking area, offering unique sandstone formations.

Boneyard: A scenic spot within The Wave area, known for its peculiar rock formations.

Paw Hole Trailhead: A hiking area leading to the visually striking Paw Hole section of South Coyote Buttes.

South Teepees at Vermilion Cliffs: Scenic spot showcasing formations that resemble teepees, with vibrant colors.

Hourglass Rock: An isolated hiking area featuring unique rock formations, including the namesake Hourglass Rock.

Ginger Rock Vortex: A unique rock formation that offers a quiet spot for visitors, often overlooked by many.

In summary…
Hiking, Camping, and Trekking in Arizona
Hiking

Arizona's hiking trails are as varied as its landscapes. The Grand Canyon, one of the world's most famous natural wonders, offers trails like the Bright Angel and South Kaibab, providing unforgettable views and challenging hikes.

Sedona's red rock paths, such as the Cathedral Rock and Devil's Bridge trails, are not only a hiker's delight but also offer some of the most picturesque landscapes in the state.

In the Flagstaff area and the White Mountains, trails lead through diverse environments, from pine forests to alpine tundras, catering to hikers looking for both beauty and solitude.

Camping

Arizona's national parks, state parks, and forests present a variety of camping experiences. Campgrounds in the Grand Canyon, Petrified Forest National Park, and Coconino National Forest, among others, offer facilities ranging from basic to fully equipped.

For those seeking a more rustic experience, backcountry camping in areas like Saguaro National Park allows for a deeper connection with the natural world. This type of camping is ideal for experiencing Arizona's stunning night skies and diverse wildlife.

Trekking

Multi-day trekking in Arizona offers an immersive experience into its unique wilderness. Extended treks through the Grand Canyon or the expansive trails of Saguaro National Park can be both challenging and rewarding.

These adventures require careful planning, from ensuring adequate supplies to obtaining necessary permits, especially in protected areas where regulations are in place to preserve the natural environment.

Adventure Sports Guide

Arizona's varied landscape, marked by rugged mountains, rolling hills, and expansive water bodies, makes it an ideal destination for a wide range of adventure sports. The state's natural terrain provides thrilling opportunities for rock climbing and bouldering, mountain biking, and various water sports.

Rock Climbing and Bouldering

Arizona is a treasure trove for climbers, with its varied geology offering numerous climbing and bouldering spots.

Mount Lemmon in Tucson boasts over 2,500 climbing routes, making it one of the largest and most diverse climbing destinations in the state. Its elevation provides cooler temperatures, making it a year-round climbing spot.

The Granite Dells in Prescott are known for their unique granite formations, offering excellent bouldering and climbing opportunities. The area's distinctive rock formations present challenges that appeal to climbers of various skill levels.

Mountain Biking

The state's diverse topography also makes it a prime location for mountain biking enthusiasts.

Sedona is world-renowned for its mountain biking trails, offering a unique experience with its scenic red rock landscapes and trails that range from easy rides to technical descents.

The **Phoenix area** has numerous trails in and around the city, suitable for riders looking for both casual rides and challenging terrain.

In the **Flagstaff region**, the high country trails provide cooler temperatures and diverse landscapes, from dense pine forests to alpine terrains, catering to bikers seeking an escape from the heat and a variety of riding experiences.

Water Sports

Despite its desert climate, Arizona offers a surprising array of water sports opportunities. The **Colorado River** is famous for its white-water rafting and kayaking, offering everything from gentle floats to challenging rapids. The river's course through the Grand Canyon provides one of the most dramatic rafting experiences in the world.

Lake Powell and **Lake Havasu** are popular for water sports such as boating, wakeboarding, and water skiing. These lakes, with their vast open waters and beautiful surroundings, are perfect for both adrenaline-fueled activities and water recreation.

Leisure and Recreational Activities

Golfing

Arizona, with its sunny weather and scenic vistas, is a golfer's paradise. The state boasts some of the best golf courses in the country, particularly in areas like Scottsdale and Phoenix.

These golf courses are known for their beautiful desert settings, innovative course designs, and impeccable maintenance. With more than 300 days of sunshine per year, golfers can enjoy year-round playing opportunities.

The courses range from highly challenging to more leisurely, ensuring that golfers of all skill levels can find a course that suits their game.

Bird Watching and Wildlife Viewing

Arizona's diverse ecosystems, from its deserts to mountain forests, support an incredible variety of bird species and wildlife, making it a prime destination for nature enthusiasts.

The southeastern part of the state is especially renowned for its bird diversity, attracting bird watchers from all over the world. Areas like the Chiricahua Mountains, Madera Canyon, and the San Pedro River Valley are hotspots for observing rare and migratory bird species.

Aside from birds, wildlife such as deer, bighorn sheep, and a variety of reptiles and mammals can be spotted throughout Arizona's national parks and wilderness areas.

Stargazing

The state's low light pollution and clear skies offer ideal conditions for stargazing and astronomical observations, particularly in remote areas.

The Grand Canyon, designated as a Dark Sky Park, provides spectacular night sky views, with organized star parties and astronomy programs for visitors.

Other notable stargazing spots include the desert regions and areas around Flagstaff, which is home to the Lowell Observatory, one of the oldest observatories in the United States.

Native American Heritage and Cultural Sites

The presence of 22 federally recognized tribes contributes to the state's rich cultural mosaic. Each tribe has its own unique traditions, art, and historical narratives, reflecting the varied experiences and histories of Native American peoples in the region. This heritage is not just a relic of the past but a living, evolving culture, integral to Arizona's identity.

Cultural Sites

The **Heard Museum** in Phoenix is a world-renowned institution dedicated to the advancement of American Indian art. It offers exhibits that both celebrate and educate about the art, history, and cultures of Native American peoples, particularly those from the Southwest.

Navajo Nation, the largest Native American reservation in the U.S., offers a glimpse into the Navajo way of life. Visitors can explore Monument Valley, Window Rock, and partake in guided tours to learn about Navajo history and culture.

The **Hopi villages** in Northern Arizona are among the oldest continuously inhabited settlements in North America. Visiting these villages offers insights into the Hopi way of life and their centuries-old traditions.

Canyon de Chelly National Monument is a site of spiritual significance to the Navajo people. The canyon walls are home to several ancient pueblo ruins, providing an understanding of the early inhabitants of the region.

Cultural Experiences

Many Native American communities in Arizona welcome visitors to learn about their cultures. These experiences often include visiting reservations, where guided tours might be available.

Pow-wows and other cultural gatherings are vibrant expressions of Native American heritage. These events are opportunities to witness traditional dances, music, and art.

Markets and Craft Fairs: Places like the Hubbell Trading Post or seasonal markets in various towns offer authentic Native American crafts, including pottery, jewelry, and textiles. These markets are not just places to purchase unique items but also to understand the artistry and symbolism behind them.

Festivals and Events Calendar
Art Festivals

Arizona's art festivals bring together local, national, and international artists, showcasing a plethora of artistic talents.

The Scottsdale Arts Festival happening **Saturday, March 23, 2024, 9 a.m. to 2 p.m. Scottsdale Family ArtsFest at SkySong** will be held on **March 22 and 23 at SkySong, The ASU Scottsdale Innovation Center** in south Scottsdale. It's a highlight, featuring artists in various mediums, from painting and sculpture to glass and ceramics. It's a place where art lovers can meet artists, purchase art, and enjoy live entertainment and workshops.

he Sedona Arts Festival is another significant event, set against the backdrop of edona's stunning red rock formations. It attracts artists and art lovers for a weekend of isual arts, live music, and culinary delights. **The oldest and largest arts festival in the erde Valley will be held on October 10 – October 11 at Sedona Red Rock High chool, 995 Upper Red Rock Loop Road, Sedona.** This incredible art festival features 25 artists from across the United States.

ultural Festivals

he state's cultural festivals celebrate the diverse backgrounds and traditions that make p Arizona's community.

he Tucson Folk Festival is a free, family-friendly event that showcases folk and roots nusic, offering performances, workshops, and jam sessions **April 5 – 7, 2024**. The ucson Folk Festival is a free and accessible festival celebrating Americana and Folk Music traditions and all the wonderful variations, including bluegrass, blues, country, jazz, Celtic, zydeco, and various styles of Latin and Mexican music.

he Arizona International Film Festival in Tucson promotes the understanding of ifferent cultures and lifestyles through the medium of film. It features a diverse range of lm genres from filmmakers around the world. The 32nd Arizona International Film estival will run from **April 17 to 28, 2024**, at exhibition venues throughout Tucson. The estival theme of Bridging Cultures provides a way to share images and voices from iverse cultures with Arizona communities. More information at
ttps://www.filmfestivalarizona.com

ocal Cuisine

he state's culinary offerings are deeply influenced by its geographical and cultural andscape.

Sonoran hot dogs, a local favorite, are a must-try. Wrapped in bacon and loaded with eans, onions, tomatoes, and various condiments, they're a testament to the region's Mexican influence.

Navajo tacos, made with fry bread instead of tortillas, offer a taste of Native American cuisine.

Chiles rellenos and other Mexican dishes are widely available and celebrated for their authenticity and richness.

Arizona's agricultural products, like citrus fruits, Medjool dates, and pecans, also play a significant role in the local cuisine, adding fresh, local flavors to various dishes.

Dining Experiences

Arizona's dining scene is as diverse as its population.

n cities like Phoenix and Scottsdale, you can find high-end dining experiences, where nnovative chefs blend traditional Southwestern flavors with contemporary culinary echniques.

Tucson, known for its vibrant Mexican food scene, offers everything from family-owned eateries serving traditional dishes to modern cafes putting a new twist on classic flavors. Roadside stands and small-town diners throughout the state provide an authentic taste of Arizona's local fare in a more casual, down-to-earth setting.

Grand Canyon and Surrounding Areas (7-Day Itinerary)

Day 1: Arrival and South Rim Exploration
- Arrive at the Grand Canyon National Park, entering through the South Entrance near Tusayan, AZ.
- Check into your accommodation at the Grand Canyon Village or Tusayan.
- Begin exploring by visiting Mather Point, one of the most iconic viewpoints of the Grand Canyon.
- Spend the afternoon walking along the Rim Trail from Mather Point to Yavapai Point and Geology Museum.
- Enjoy dinner at one of the restaurants in the Grand Canyon Village.

Day 2: South Rim Hiking and Scenic Drives
- Start early with a hike down the Bright Angel Trail; go as far as you're comfortable, but remember you have to hike back up.
- In the afternoon, take a scenic drive along the Desert View Drive, stopping at major viewpoints like Grandview Point and Moran Point.
- End the day at Desert View Watchtower for panoramic views and sunset.
- Return to the village for dinner and rest.

Day 3: North Rim Visit
- Drive to the North Rim (this can take 4-5 hours, so start early). Note: North Rim is seasonal, typically open mid-May to mid-October.
- Visit the North Rim Visitor Center and take in the different perspective of the Grand Canyon from Bright Angel Point.
- Hike a portion of the North Kaibab Trail or take a leisurely walk on the Transept Trail.
- Enjoy a sunset at Cape Royal before returning to your North Rim accommodation.

Day 4: More North Rim Exploration
- Spend another day exploring the North Rim. Consider a hike on the Widforss Trail for a mix of forest and canyon views.
- Relax at the Grand Canyon Lodge, taking in the views from the patio or the Sun Room.
- Drive to Point Imperial, the highest viewpoint in the park, for different scenery and photo opportunities.
- Return to lodge or campsite for the evening.

Day 5: Rafting or Scenic Flight
- Return to the South Rim or stay in Page, AZ (if you opted for a scenic flight from there).
- Book a half-day or full-day rafting trip on the Colorado River or a scenic helicopter or airplane tour over the canyon (reserve in advance).
- Spend the afternoon relaxing and reflecting on the aerial or river perspective of the canyon.
- Enjoy another peaceful night at the South Rim or Page.

Day 6: Hiking and Educational Programs
- Spend the day engaging in less strenuous activities. Visit the Grand Canyon Visitor Center and attend a ranger-led talk or walk.
- Hike along the Rim Trail or explore the trail to Shoshone Point, a less crowded viewpoint.

- Visit the historic Grand Canyon Railway Station and Kolb Studio.
- Watch the sunset from Hopi Point, known for its wide-ranging views.

Day 7: Leisure and Departure
- Enjoy a leisurely morning at the South Rim. Take any last-minute photos and visit any souvenir shops.
- Consider a short walk on the Trail of Time to learn about the canyon's geological history.
- Check out of your accommodation and begin your journey back home, or to your next destination.

Phoenix and Surroundings (7-Day Itinerary)
Day 1: Downtown Phoenix and Cultural Exploration
- Start your day exploring the Phoenix Art Museum and the Heard Museum to immerse yourself in art and culture.
- Enjoy lunch at a downtown restaurant featuring Southwestern cuisine.
- Spend the afternoon at the Arizona Science Center or the Children's Museum of Phoenix, depending on your interest.
- Dine in the Roosevelt Row Arts District and enjoy the vibrant street art and galleries.

Day 2: Desert Botanical Garden and Camelback Mountain
- Visit the Desert Botanical Garden in the morning to see the beautiful desert plants.
- Have a picnic lunch in the garden or dine at the garden's cafe.
- In the afternoon, hike Camelback Mountain for panoramic views of the city (choose Echo Canyon Trail or Cholla Trail based on your hiking level).
- Relax with a casual dinner and perhaps catch a performance at the Phoenix Theatre or the Orpheum Theater.

Day 3: South Mountain Park and Heritage Square
- Spend the morning exploring South Mountain Park, one of the largest municipal parks in the United States. Choose from various trails for hiking or mountain biking.
- Have lunch at a café in the area, then head to Heritage Square to explore historic Phoenix.
- Tour the Rosson House Museum and learn about Phoenix's Victorian past.
- Enjoy dinner at one of the Heritage Square restaurants or explore the culinary scene in downtown Phoenix.

Day 4: Day Trip to Scottsdale
- Take a day trip to nearby Scottsdale. Start with a visit to Old Town Scottsdale to shop and explore the art galleries.
- Have lunch at one of Old Town's many eateries.
- In the afternoon, visit the Scottsdale Museum of Contemporary Art and walk through the Civic Center Mall.
- Return to Phoenix and dine at a restaurant offering views of the city skyline.

Day 5: Phoenix Zoo and Papago Park
- Visit the Phoenix Zoo in the morning and enjoy the wildlife exhibits.
- Have a picnic lunch in Papago Park, then explore the park's trails, the Hole-in-the-Rock formation, and the nearby Hall of Flame Fire Museum.
- Spend a leisurely afternoon at the Phoenix Municipal Stadium or go fishing in one of the park's ponds.

- Dine in the nearby Tempe area or head back to Phoenix for dinner.

Day 6: Museums and Historical Sites

- Spend your day exploring Phoenix's museums such as the Pueblo Grande Museum and Archaeological Park, and the Arizona Capitol Museum.
- Have lunch in the Capitol area and then visit the Wesley Bolin Memorial Plaza.
- In the afternoon, explore the Wrigley Mansion for a tour of the historic estate.
- Enjoy dinner at a restaurant that highlights Arizona's local ingredients and flavors.

Day 7: Relaxation and Leisure

- Spend your last day relaxing. Start with a leisurely breakfast or brunch at a popular Phoenix café.
- Visit a spa for a massage or treatment, or simply lounge by a pool.
- Spend your afternoon shopping at Biltmore Fashion Park or exploring the boutiques and shops in central Phoenix.
- Enjoy a farewell dinner at one of Phoenix's top restaurants, reflecting on your week in the city.

Tucson and Surroundings (7-Day Itinerary)

Day 1: Downtown Tucson Exploration

- Start your day with breakfast at a local café.
- Visit the Tucson Museum of Art and Historic Block to immerse yourself in regional art and history.
- Stroll through El Presidio Historic District and see the old adobe architecture.
- Have lunch at one of the downtown Mexican restaurants.
- In the afternoon, explore the unique shops and galleries in the Fourth Avenue District.
- Finish your day with dinner at a downtown restaurant and enjoy local Southwestern cuisine.

Day 2: Nature and Science Day

- Start your morning at the Arizona-Sonora Desert Museum, a blend of zoo, botanical garden, art gallery, and natural history museum.
- Have lunch at the museum's café.
- In the afternoon, visit the Kitt Peak National Observatory or the Flandrau Science Center & Planetarium, depending on your interest in astronomy.
- Return to Tucson for dinner, perhaps trying a different regional cuisine.

Day 3: Historical and Cultural Discovery

- Visit Mission San Xavier del Bac in the morning and explore this historic Spanish mission.
- Head back towards Tucson and stop for lunch at a local eatery.
- Spend your afternoon at the Pima Air & Space Museum, exploring one of the world's largest aircraft collections.
- For dinner, experience some live music and local dining in the downtown area or check out a show at the Fox Tucson Theatre.

Day 4: Outdoor Adventure

- Start early and head to Sabino Canyon for a morning of hiking or a tram ride through the beautiful desert landscape.
- Enjoy a picnic lunch in the canyon or dine at a nearby café.

- Spend the afternoon at the Tucson Botanical Gardens, exploring the diverse plant life and butterfly greenhouse.
- Relax in the evening with a leisurely dinner at one of Tucson's fine dining establishments.

Day 5: Art and Culture
- Begin your day exploring the University of Arizona campus, visiting the UA Art Museum and the Center for Creative Photography.
- Have lunch on or near campus, enjoying a variety of dining options.
- In the afternoon, visit the DeGrazia Gallery in the Sun, a historic art gallery set in the beautiful desert.
- For dinner, explore the culinary scene in the Mercado San Agustin or the MSA Annex.

Day 6: Culinary and Heritage Tour
- Join a Tucson food tour in the morning to taste your way through the city's culinary heritage.
- Spend your afternoon in Barrio Viejo, appreciating the historic adobe architecture and local art scene.
- Have dinner at one of the many Mexican restaurants, trying traditional dishes like Sonoran hot dogs or carne seca.

Day 7: Leisure and Shopping
- Enjoy a relaxed morning with brunch at a local café.
- Spend your day shopping for souvenirs and local crafts at La Encantada or the Lost Barrio shopping districts.
- Visit the Reid Park Zoo or relax in one of Tucson's city parks if you're looking for a slower pace.
- Conclude your trip with a farewell dinner at a restaurant with views of the desert sunset.

Sedona and Surroundings (7-Day Itinerary)
Day 1: Arrival and Downtown Sedona
- Arrive in Sedona and check into your hotel.
- Spend the afternoon exploring Uptown Sedona and Tlaquepaque Arts & Shopping Village.
- Have dinner at one of Sedona's restaurants, enjoying local Southwestern cuisine.
- Attend a stargazing event or simply enjoy the star-filled night sky from your accommodation.

Day 2: Red Rock Exploration and Hiking
- Start your day with a hike. Consider trails like Devil's Bridge, Cathedral Rock, or Bell Rock for iconic Sedona views.
- Pack a picnic lunch or return to town for a meal.
- Spend the afternoon relaxing or visit the Sedona Heritage Museum to learn about the area's history.
- Enjoy a casual dinner, then explore local art galleries or attend a live music event.

Day 3: Spiritual Journey and Vortex Experience
- Begin your day with a spiritual or wellness activity, such as a guided vortex tour, yoga, or meditation class.
- Visit the Chapel of the Holy Cross and spend time reflecting in its serene setting.

- Have lunch in town, then spend the afternoon at the Amitabha Stupa & Peace Park for a peaceful hike and meditation.
- Dine at a restaurant with views of the red rocks, then consider booking a nighttime spiritual or UFO tour.

Day 4: Scenic Drives and Wine Tasting
- Take a scenic drive along the Red Rock Scenic Byway (SR 179) and the Oak Creek Canyon Scenic Drive (SR 89A).
- Stop at Oak Creek Vista for breathtaking views and local crafts.
- Head to Page Springs/Cornville for wine tasting at local vineyards and wineries.
- Return to Sedona for dinner, perhaps choosing a venue offering local wines.

Day 5: Water Activities and Relaxation
- Spend the morning kayaking, tubing, or swimming in Oak Creek.
- Enjoy a leisurely lunch by the creek.
- In the afternoon, book a spa treatment or visit a wellness center for relaxation and rejuvenation.
- Have a quiet dinner and enjoy a peaceful evening under the Sedona sky.

Day 6: Adventure Day
- Choose an adventure activity: Jeep tour, mountain biking, rock climbing, or a hot air balloon ride.
- Have a relaxing lunch and perhaps explore more of the town or visit an art studio.
- Spend the afternoon at leisure; consider a gentle hike or a visit to another vortex site.
- For your last evening, enjoy a special meal at one of Sedona's fine dining restaurants, or participate in a cooking class if available.

Day 7: Last Day Reflections and Departure
- Start your day with a gentle walk or a final meditation session to reflect on your Sedona experience.
- Visit any shops or sites you may have missed or return to a place that resonated with you during your stay.
- Enjoy a farewell lunch in Sedona, then prepare for your departure.

Flagstaff and Surroundings (7-Day Itinerary)
Day 1: Discover Downtown Flagstaff
- Begin with breakfast at a downtown café.
- Explore the historic downtown area, visiting local shops and the Heritage Square.
- Have lunch at one of the local breweries or eateries.
- Spend the afternoon at the Museum of Northern Arizona.
- Enjoy dinner downtown, then catch a performance at the Orpheum Theater or enjoy live music at one of the local bars.

Day 2: Outdoor Adventure and Scenic Views
- Start early and spend the day at the Walnut Canyon National Monument, exploring ancient cliff dwellings and hiking the trails.
- Pack a picnic lunch to enjoy amidst the canyon's natural beauty.
- Return to Flagstaff and dine at a restaurant offering views of the San Francisco Peaks.
- If energy permits, end your day with a stargazing session at Lowell Observatory.

Day 3: Grand Canyon Day Trip

Dedicate this day to visiting the Grand Canyon National Park, about a 90-minute drive from Flagstaff.

Enjoy the scenic drive, stop at various viewpoints, and take short hikes along the rim.

Have lunch at one of the park's restaurants or pack a picnic.

Return to Flagstaff for a relaxing dinner.

Day 4: Cultural and Historical Insights

Spend your morning at the Riordan Mansion State Historic Park.

Enjoy lunch at a local café.

In the afternoon, visit the Pioneer Museum or the Arizona Historical Society Pioneer Museum to learn about Flagstaff's history.

Dine downtown and consider visiting the Flagstaff Brewing Company for a taste of local beer.

Day 5: Nature Day

Start with a hike or bike ride on the Flagstaff Urban Trails System.

Have a relaxing lunch in town.

Spend the afternoon at the Arboretum at Flagstaff or take a scenic drive on the San Francisco Peaks.

For dinner, try one of Flagstaff's farm-to-table restaurants.

Day 6: Explore Surrounding Natural Wonders

Visit the Lava River Cave in the morning—bring warm clothes and flashlights.

Enjoy lunch at a café back in Flagstaff.

In the afternoon, head to the Coconino National Forest for hiking, wildlife viewing, or simply enjoying nature.

Have dinner at a Flagstaff restaurant with a view, or opt for a campfire meal if you're up for more outdoor time.

Day 7: Relaxation and Leisure

Start with a leisurely brunch at one of Flagstaff's local spots.

Visit the Northern Arizona University campus and explore its art galleries or take a self-guided tour.

Spend your afternoon enjoying leisure activities such as golfing, spa treatments, or shopping for souvenirs.

Conclude your Flagstaff experience with a farewell dinner at one of the city's finest restaurants, reflecting on your week's adventures.

Maps and Navigation

Printed Maps

Printed maps are invaluable, especially in remote areas where cell service may be spotty.

Arizona State Road Map: Available at visitor centers and through the Arizona Department of Transportation, this map provides a comprehensive view of the state's highways and roads.

Trail Maps: For specific hiking areas like the Grand Canyon, Sedona, or the White Mountains, trail maps are available at local visitor centers or outdoor stores. These are crucial for safe hiking and understanding the terrain.

Online Maps and Apps

Google Maps: Useful for route planning and finding points of interest, like restaurants, gas stations, and accommodations. Always download maps for offline use when exploring remote areas.

AllTrails: A popular app for hiking trails, providing detailed trail maps, user reviews, and the ability to track your hike.

The Dyrt: Helpful for finding and reviewing campgrounds, including amenities and access details.

GPS Navigation Systems

GPS devices are reliable for road trips, especially in areas without cell service. Consider renting a GPS device if your car doesn't have one built-in.

Specialized Maps

Topographic Maps: For backcountry adventures and trekking, topographic maps from the US Geological Survey (USGS) are beneficial.

National Park Service Maps: The NPS provides detailed maps of national parks, including the Grand Canyon, Petrified Forest, and Saguaro National Park.

Important Laws and Traveler Responsibilities
Traffic Laws

Speed Limits

Speed limits in Arizona vary depending on the type of road and the area. For instance, in urban areas, speed limits might range from 25 to 45 mph, while on rural highways, they can be as high as 65 to 75 mph.

Always look for and adhere to posted speed limit signs. Speed limits are enforced to ensure safety, especially in areas with heavy traffic or challenging road conditions.

Seat Belt Laws

Arizona requires all front-seat occupants to wear seat belts. This law is intended to reduce the risk of injury in case of an accident.

For children under 8 years old, Arizona law mandates the use of an appropriate child safety seat. The specifics may vary based on the child's age, height, and weight, so it's important to use a seat that's appropriate for your child's size.

DUI Laws

Driving Under the Influence (DUI) is taken very seriously in Arizona. The state has strict laws and penalties for those found driving with a Blood Alcohol Content (BAC) of 0.08% or higher. Even lower levels of alcohol can result in a DUI charge if it's determined that the alcohol has impaired your ability to drive. Penalties for DUI can include fines, jail time, mandatory alcohol education programs, and suspension of your driver's license. Remember, the safest policy is not to drive at all after consuming alcohol or drugs that could impair your driving ability.

Environmental Protection

Littering

Littering is not only harmful to the environment but is also illegal in Arizona. It can lead to significant fines. Always dispose of trash in designated receptacles. If none are available, carry your trash with you until you can dispose of it properly. This also applies to smaller items like cigarette butts and food wrappers, which can be harmful to wildlife and the natural landscape.

Wildlife Interactions
Feeding wildlife disrupts their natural foraging habits and can lead to health problems for the animals and safety issues for humans. Maintain a respectful distance from wildlife. This not only protects the animals but also ensures your safety, as even seemingly docile animals can be unpredictable. Use binoculars or a zoom lens for a closer look at animals without disturbing them.

Trail and Park Regulations
Staying on designated trails helps to protect fragile ecosystems and prevent erosion. Venturing off-trail can damage plant life and disturb wildlife habitats. National parks, forests, and other protected areas have specific rules designed to protect these environments. These may include regulations on camping, fires, and recreational activities.

Be mindful of signs and notices that inform visitors of the regulations in each area. This can include rules specific to certain trails, areas where pets are not allowed, and zones designated for specific activities.

Alcohol and Smoking Regulations

Legal Drinking Age: In Arizona, as in the rest of the United States, the legal age for alcohol consumption is 21 years. It is important to carry a valid ID for age verification when purchasing or consuming alcohol.

Public Consumption of Alcohol: Drinking alcohol in public places is generally prohibited, except in designated areas like licensed bars, restaurants, or specific events where alcohol consumption is allowed.

Smoking Regulations: Smoking is banned in most enclosed public places and workplaces, including bars and restaurants. This law is intended to protect people from secondhand smoke. Be sure to check for designated smoking areas and always be considerate of non-smokers.

Drone Use: Drones are increasingly popular for photography and recreation, but it's essential to follow the Federal Aviation Administration (FAA) rules. This includes not flying drones near airports, in national parks, or over private property without permission. Always check local regulations, as some areas may have specific rules or restrictions on drone use.

Arizona is committed to providing accessible travel facilities and services to ensure that all visitors, including those with disabilities, can enjoy their experience. Here's an overview of accessible travel options and services in the state:

Transportation

Airports: Major airports in Arizona, like Phoenix Sky Harbor and Tucson International, are equipped with accessibility features such as wheelchair ramps, accessible restrooms, and assistance services.

Public Transportation: Many cities in Arizona offer accessible public transportation options, including buses and light rail systems with features like low-floor entry and designated seating for passengers with disabilities.

Accommodations

Hotels and resorts across Arizona offer accessible rooms and facilities. These may include features like wheelchair-accessible bathrooms, grab bars, and visual alert systems. It's advisable to confirm specific accessibility needs when booking.

Attractions and Parks

Grand Canyon National Park: Offers accessible viewpoints, shuttle buses, and trails, such as the Rim Trail, which has paved sections suitable for wheelchairs.

State and National Parks: Many have accessible trails, picnic areas, and visitor centers. For instance, Saguaro National Park and Petrified Forest National Park have accessible features and exhibits.

Museums and Cultural Sites: Places like the Heard Museum, Arizona-Sonora Desert Museum, and Phoenix Art Museum are accessible, offering features like wheelchair ramps and accessible restrooms.

Outdoor Activities

Arizona offers a range of accessible outdoor activities. Companies provide adaptive hiking, kayaking, and other outdoor experiences tailored for individuals with disabilities. Some parks offer accessible camping options, with facilities like raised fire grates and accessible restrooms.

Assistance Services

Visitor centers and major tourist attractions often have information available about local accessibility services, including equipment rental (wheelchairs, scooters), and specialized tour operators. Service animals are generally welcome in most public areas and accommodations.

Useful Resources

The Arizona Office of Tourism provides information on accessible travel and can be a valuable resource for planning your trip. Websites like Accessible Arizona https://www.visitarizona.com/plan/accessibility offer insights and tips for travelers with disabilities.

138

Itinerary Planner

Destination :   **Travel Date :**

DAY

Destination :
Budget :
☐ Tickets
☐ Print Voucher

DAY

Destination :
Budget :
☐ Tickets
☐ Print Voucher

DAY

Destination :
Budget :
☐ Tickets
☐ Print Voucher

DAY

Destination :
Budget :
☐ Tickets
☐ Print Voucher

DAY

Destination :
Budget :
☐ Tickets
☐ Print Voucher

Itinerary Planner

Destination :   **Travel Date :**

DAY

Destination :
Budget :
☐ Tickets
☐ Print Voucher

DAY

Destination :
Budget :
☐ Tickets
☐ Print Voucher

DAY

Destination :
Budget :
☐ Tickets
☐ Print Voucher

DAY

Destination :
Budget :
☐ Tickets
☐ Print Voucher

DAY

Destination :
Budget :
☐ Tickets
☐ Print Voucher

NOTES

Printed in Great Britain
by Amazon

40432533R00086